Adaptive Marketing

Adaptive Marketing

Leveraging Real-Time Data to Become a More Competitive and Successful Company

Norm Johnston

First published in 2015 by
PALGRAVE MACMILLAN®
in the United States—a division of St. Martin's Press LLC,
175 Fifth Avenue, New York, NY 10010.

Where this book is distributed in the UK, Europe and the rest of the world,
this is by Palgrave Macmillan, a division of Macmillan Publishers Limited,
registered in England, company number 785998, of Houndmills,
Basingstoke, Hampshire RG21 6XS.

Palgrave Macmillan is the global academic imprint of the above companies
and has companies and representatives throughout the world.

Palgrave® and Macmillan® are registered trademarks in the United States,
the United Kingdom, Europe and other countries.

ISBN: 978–1–137–46292–3

Library of Congress Cataloging-in-Publication Data

Johnston, Norm.
   Adaptive marketing : leveraging real-time data to become a more competitive
and successful company / Norm Johnston.
      pages cm
   ISBN 978–1–137–46292–3 (alk. paper)
      1. Internet marketing. 2. Marketing—Data processes. I. Title.

HF5415.1265.J64 2015
658.8—dc23   2015012373

 A catalogue record of the book is available from the British Library.

Design by Newgen Knowledge Works (P) Ltd., Chennai, India.

First edition: September 2015

10 9 8 7 6 5 4 3 2 1

Printed in the United States of America.

Contents

Figures

Foreword

Norm Johnston's *Adaptive Marketing* successfully articulates the impact of the digital age on the velocity of marketing. Marketing has changed. For generations strategies were conceived, messages were created and delivered in just a few channels, and marketers and agencies alike waited. They waited for tracking studies to illuminate levels of awareness and preference and waited longer still to receive the orders that told them to start the line and deliver more of their product to customers. Periods of minimal illumination stretched between phases, and marketers were largely impotent in reacting to threats or opportunities with new messaging, altered weight, timing, or location of delivery.

The adaptive marketer knows more, knows it more quickly, and responds to greater effect. She knows what works and what does not; she knows where it works and where it does not; she knows more about her customer and can refine her delivery to optimize shareholder value and market share.

The adaptive marketer's greatest ally is data, not just the slow moving data of generations past but fast moving data and signals that indicate opportunities for new revenues, customer sentiment, geographic or demographic pockets of opportunity, and, of course, sales. From social media to point of sale, from search queries to e-mail response, from online sales to weather, the adaptive marketer can listen, analyze, and respond in an approximation to real time.

The Internet, in all its mobile, social, local, searchable, addressable, countable (and sometimes accountable) features has unlocked potential for precise actions at great speed.

Of course, marketers have always been adaptive. They combined the foundational layer of media—long-time channels as diverse as broadcast television, *Out of Home* and other consumer magazines—with newspapers, radio, and other channels with compressed timetables from concept to air date. Adaptive channels these may be, but they offer only a pale comparison to the opportunities presented today.

For the most part, digital advertising inventory is unlimited, production cycles have accelerated, and the time from "moment" to tweet is just that, a moment. Across the spectrum of digital advertising inventory, programmatic delivery of communications is becoming prevalent, combined with technologies that enable dynamic creative messaging and the sources of insight that can inform that message.

We are part of a new generation of marketers who are simply using data to move forward very, very fast.

ROB NORMAN,
Chief Digital Officer,
GroupM

Acknowledgments

Winston Churchill once said, "To improve is to change, to be perfect is to change often." In the true spirit of being adaptive, this book has certainly evolved and changed since I first started typing the first few sentences. I'm certain it's not perfect, but I hope you find it informative, insightful, and inspirational.

Writing at its extreme can be a very solitary experience consisting of countless hours hunched over a laptop on long airplane rides, rainy Sunday afternoons, even random spare moments scattered throughout an otherwise busy professional and personal life. It can be hard work at times, often alleviated by listening to Miles Davis, in other cases spurred on by the support of many, many others.

One such person is my editor Laurie Harting and her team at Palgrave Macmillan, including Marcus Ballenger, who have been so encouraging and helpful every step of the way. Whether reviewing the formatting or advising on the content, they have been indispensable in making it all happen. Laurie, thank you for giving me the opportunity and keeping me motivated along the journey, particularly during the crunch times. This book simply wouldn't have happened without you.

Thanks also to my colleagues at Mindshare, GroupM, and WPP who have helped in a myriad of ways. You inspire me every day with great thinking and great work. Special thanks to Nick Emery for his confidence in me, leadership, and permission to write the book. I'm eternally grateful to Rob Norman for his wisdom and wit and for agreeing to write the foreword. And I have to acknowledge all those incredibly talented people I work with every day around the world who have embraced adaptive marketing in so many different ways in so many different places. A shout-out to Greg Brooks for his advice on everything from covers to content and to Simeon Duckworth for sitting next to me at work and putting up with my never-ending adaptive claptrap.

Gracias, merci, danke to all of the interviewees and essay contributors from around the world who I pursued and cajoled everywhere from Vegas to Coventry: Rob Norman, Chris Whalen, Eileen Naughton, Tom Buday, Pete Blackshaw, Keith Weed, Luis di Como, Jeff Cole, Nathan Summers, Preston Reed, Laurent Burman, Curt Hecht, Caspar Schlickum, John Montgomery, Vikesh Shah, Jim Downing, Jeffrey Rohrs, Brian Wong, Barry Kahn, Steve Mannel, Eric Frankel, Yolanda Lam, Chris Glode, Mort Greenberg, and Justin DeGeorge. If I've accidently omitted anyone, my apologies and a promise to make it up somehow.

A very special thanks to the formidable April Wardy, who has worked harder than anyone to support me on this book. April enthusiastically collected mountains of research, piously maintained version control through the editing process, chased permissions and agreements, and made every table and chart look perfect. Thank you, April, for everything you have done, all the hard work, and for smiling throughout the entire process.

And a final big thanks to my family. To my parents Norm and Diane who raised me in Ohio and taught me the value of a decent education, good values, and hard work. To my father-in-law Gilbert for all the Leffes and laughs. To my Uncle Joe for being the ultimate storyteller, and my Aunt Jan and Uncle Jon for always being there. To my siblings Jason and Jill for just being cool. To my wonderful wife Chantal for her love, support, and patience, particularly when I disappeared for a few hours during the weekend to write some more. To my three boys Thomas, Nicolas, and Benjamin who keep me young in spirit but also knowledgeable about the latest and greatest technology. I'm so lucky to be your son, nephew, sibling, husband, and father.

CHAPTER 1

A Few Words about Data

Z is for Zettabyte

For those of you seeking some interesting trivia for an upcoming bar debate or dinner party conversation, let me introduce you to the awesomeness of the mighty zettabyte.

The zettabyte is a member of the byte family, that long-standing unit of digital information made up of eight little bits. Think of it as the computing version of the real world's atom and its tiny quarks. Both are, as far as we know today, the smallest addressable units in their respective worlds, one in the virtual world and one in the physical world.

What's so special about a zettabyte? Well, it's big, really big. In fact, one zettabyte is approximately 1,000,000,000,000,000,000,000 bytes or, if you want to shorten that, about 1,000 exabytes or one billion terabytes. Any way you measure it, a zettabyte is a lot of bytes.

The zettabyte is a relative newcomer to our world, so be nice to it. Way back in 2006, all the world's combined data storage space equaled about 160 exabytes or a measly 0.16 of a zettabyte. Fast forward a few years, and with an ever-expanding Internet, we now have a whole lot more bytes in the world. In fact, as of 2013, we had roughly 4.4 zettabytes of data storage space taken up by everything from Netflix videos to Amazon Wish Lists to Facebook news feeds.[1] Google's executive chairman, Eric Schmidt, boasted back in 2003 that "every two days we create as much information as we did from the dawn of civilization up until 2003."[2] In fact, Google's YouTube is a major zettabyte contributor; at the moment, over 300 hours of video are uploaded to YouTube every minute.[3] After thousands of years of civilization, within a few short years our world has produced over 90 percent of the data that the planet has ever known.[4]

Impressive, but nothing compared to what lies ahead. Consider what multinational technology and data services provider EMC Corporation and global marketing intelligence firm International Data Corporation (IDC) estimate will happen in the near future. These companies estimate that our digital universe of data will increase to 44 zettabytes in the next few years (see Figure 1.1). That's right, 44 of those big zettabytes compared to today's four. To give you some perspective: according to EMC, if you put all of those 44 zettabytes worth of data on DVDs, you could stack them all the way to the moon and back. It's a vast amount of data, roughly the equivalent to the amount of

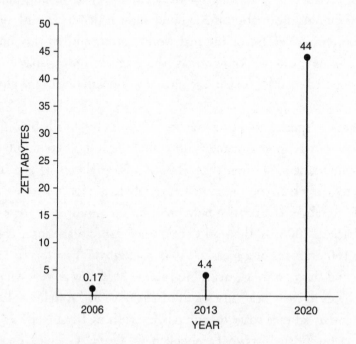

Figure 1.1   Forecasted Growth in the World's Total Data.
Source: IDC, 2014.

information that would be generated by everyone in the world posting messages on Twitter continuously for a century.

So, get comfortable with our new friend, the zettabyte. Whether you like it or not, there is a data tsunami heading in your direction. It's now just a question of how you will use it.

Human Data Emissions

Where are these mighty zettabytes coming from? For the moment, mostly from you, particularly if you are one of the 3 billion people currently on the Internet.[5] In fact, every day you are leaving a trail of data exhaust emanating from your Internet usage. Like a plane flying across a clear sky, you leave a large stream of data behind in the clouds, but in this case the stream is in the Internet's virtual cloud rather than in the physical kind.

And you are about to be joined by many others. According to most industry estimates, around 3 billion more people will officially become permanent and sustained members of the Internet for the first time. Many of these Internet newbies will convert once that magical digital trifecta occurs in their particular market: cheaper, IP-enabled smart phones; low-cost or flat-priced Internet broadband; and, finally, decent and relevant content (see Figure 1.2). Of course, this digital trifecta will be assisted by companies with a vested interest in continuing to expand their businesses.

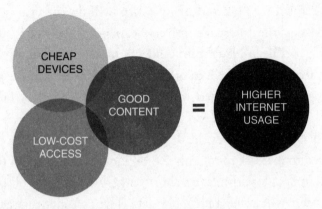

Figure 1.2 Variables That Lead to Higher Internet Usage.

Two Silicon Valley giants come to mind. Facebook's internet.org is a prime example of this "win-win" approach. Internet.org will bring together a multitude of companies, including handset manufacturers and telecommunication carriers, to bring cheap Internet access to millions who are without it today. Naturally, Facebook will be one of the preinstalled applications, thus helping that company to expand its user base beyond the current 1.5 billion and sell more advertising in the process.

Google has its equivalent effort, including Project Loon, which aims to provide Internet access to remote regions of the world by balloons. Google also recently launched its Android One phone in an effort to equip more consumers with smartphones; according to Google, currently only one in four people have a smartphone. Android One makes it cheaper for manufacturers to create smartphones as it provides a basic turnkey operating system experience priced around $100. Android One launched in India in 2014, with future expansion planned in Indonesia, the Philippines, Sri Lanka, and other South Asian markets. However, Google isn't just supporting developing countries; it is also pushing for better bandwidth in its home market. Google is busy tearing up roads everywhere from Utah to North Carolina as part of its Fiber service, which gives consumers Internet access at speeds that are more than 100 times faster than today's average. Google Fiber can reach up to 1 gigabyte per second, enabling consumers to conduct faster searches and watch more videos than ever before.

Google and Facebook and many others will do everything in their power to keep the Internet's universe expanding, as their businesses depend on it. Eileen Naughton, Google's managing director and vice president for the United Kingdom and Ireland, explains: "It's good for more people to be connected to the Internet. It's good for humanity, and it's also good for business."[6]

Regardless of who solves the digital trifecta, the Internet population is predicted to increase to roughly 5.8 billion, or 83 percent of the planet's 7 billion people within a few short years.[7] And with all of these new Internet users will come a lot more data. Just consider that according to the United Kingdom's *Guardian* newspaper, the average consumer drops around 3,254 pieces of data into a database each week. Now multiply that figure by an extra 3 billion people and you can see why we are talking about zettabytes rather than exabytes.

Arguably the biggest change with these new 3 billion users will be the way they access the Internet. Many will simply skip the PC altogether, quickly moving to mobile devices as their primary or indeed only Internet device. For example, in China, 70 percent of new Internet users use mobile devices only,[8] frequently cheap, high-quality smartphones from home-grown companies such as Xiaomi. According to IMS Research, smartphone sales in China will more than quadruple between 2010 and 2016 to reach 400 million units by 2016.[9] Likewise in neighboring India, smartphone usage is growing steadily if not staggeringly. According to a recent study, there are 51 million smartphone users in urban India today, an 89 percent increase from 2012, when there were just 27 million users.[10] And in Africa, Kenya's M-PESA mobile financial transaction service is now used by over 17 million Kenyans; this is the equivalent of more than two-thirds of the adult population. M-PESA is so pervasive in the country that 25 percent of the country's gross national product flows through it.[11] All of these trends are underlined by Morgan Stanley's claim that mobile Internet use has surpassed PC Internet usage for the first time in 2014 (see Figure 1.3).

Consequently, we won't just see more Internet users, we will also see a very different type of Internet use, one that in the words of Google's Naughton, will provide many more "portable and ubiquitous data points" as people use their smartphones throughout the day. Cisco's Global Mobile Data Traffic Forecast reveals just how fast we are progressing from a relatively slow, expensive mobile Internet experience to an increasingly high-speed infrastructure. According to Cisco, smartphones will reach 66 percent of total mobile data traffic by 2018, most of this will be juiced up by faster connection speeds like 3G, which will increase twofold during this time. In some markets, 4G will gain even more traction. Traffic at 4G will be more than half of the total mobile traffic by 2018; even though it will only make up 15 percent of mobile connections.[12] The result will be a massive increase in mobile data traffic, which, according to Cisco, will grow at a compound annual growth

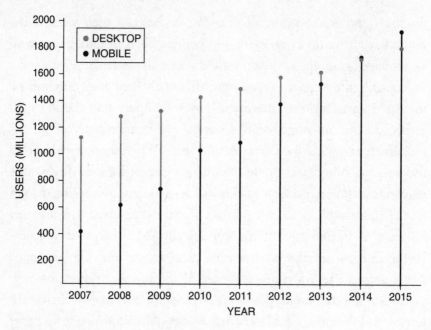

Figure 1.3 Mobile Internet Users Surpasses PC Users.
Source: Morgan Stanley 2010.

rate of 61 percent between 2013 and 2018. By 2018, mobile-connected tablets will generate nearly double the traffic generated by the entire global mobile network in 2013.

In short, many more users, mostly on mobile devices, providing a nonstop stream of real-time data cumulating into all those zettabytes. Now we know why the industry calls it "big data." However, there is more to this story than just size.

An UnBeliebable Story

Just when you were warming up to zettabytes and the power of so-called big data, it might be time to take a step back and consider some of the other advantages of data beyond its size. In fact, when it comes to data, there are several other factors that can give it immense power for marketers.

First, data now comes to us at immense speed. It's really swift. In the old analog world getting data was often a laborious, slow process. Think of questionnaires posted through the mail system, catalogues dropped on door steps, and shelves stacked with volumes of the *Encyclopaedia Britannica*. IP-enabled devices now give consumers instant access to all types of information. Saturday night dinner party debates are no longer researched and concluded the following week; now they are resolved instantly via Google on a smartphone. Sometimes this velocity with data can have unexpected results, both positive and negative.

Take the #BaldforBieber incident in late 2012. A story swiftly circulated on social networks such as Facebook and Twitter that the young Canadian rock star Justin Bieber had been diagnosed with cancer and was undergoing chemotherapy, which had resulted in the singer losing his hair. Whatever your feelings may be about enfant terrible Bieber, it was a sad story, and naturally his fans quickly responded to the news. When I say fans, I mean lots of fans; Bieber has over 50 million "Beliebers" on Twitter alone, and many of them used the hashtag #BaldforBieber to send best wishes and support for the ailing singer. Some fans even went so far as to go bald themselves to show solidarity and sympathy and posted videos on YouTube of themselves shaving off their hair. The #BaldforBieber cause went on unabated for several days until finally Justin Bieber's bodyguard set the record straight. In reality, Justin was absolutely fine, and any news of him battling cancer was completely untrue. Both his health and his hair were perfectly intact. In fact, the entire story was a hoax from the well-known pranksters at the Internet site 4Chan, who had planted the story using a fake photoshopped tweet from the US TV show *Entertainment Tonight*. Unfortunately, by the time the record was set straight four days after the story broke, there was already a legion of newly bald Beliebers around the world, many of whom had already posted their bald head videos on YouTube.

The speed of today's flow of data has been greatly increased by a dramatic increase in social sharing by consumers. One could argue that data has always flowed socially, whether at the local pub or over the telephone. What has changed with the Internet is simply the scale of social data as consumers can now instantly pass information and content to *many* more people. Facebook alone connects at least 1.5 billion people. In fact, there's no point in referencing the specific number of users on the social network as it will be outdated within seconds. Let's just say it's a very big number.

Other social networks continue to grow, including applications such as Twitter with nearly 300 million registered users and counting and China's WeChat with over 500 million users and growing. In addition to these mega networks, a wide variety of other social apps are also flourishing, including Instagram, SnapChat, Tumblr, and Sina Weibo.

What's most notable about these social applications is not so much the networks themselves but how they have become so ubiquitous in the broader Internet ecosystem. Rather than stand-alone and siloed social hubs, Facebook Like buttons and Twitter retweet buttons are now embedded all over the web. In effect, the Internet has become one giant social network, with pretty much every piece of content instantly shareable with your friends. Facebook calls it "Social by Design," which essentially means developing your content so that it can be easily socialized with your social graph, which is its fancy way of saying that it can be shared with your friends. According to publically released information from its Data Science group, Facebook alone is producing around 2.5 billion pieces of content and over 500 terabytes of data each day. In effect, it's now easier than ever to swiftly share information, including stories about brands, even false ones.

Such false news stories have become much more common as social networks have grown. The stories can be created by everyday consumers, pranksters, special interest groups with a bone to pick, or the many satire news sites such as the *Onion* or *Nipsys News*. While the later sites clearly flag brand-related satire stories as false, once shared with others a story can quickly become accepted as fact. Like a virtual game of Chinese whispers, the original message can quickly morph into something entirely different after it's been passed on several times.

Take Wave, a purportedly new Apple service that was widely "advertised" and shared on various Apple forums and social networks. This new service, as featured in a nicely executed advertisement mocked-up in Apple's trademark style, enabled you to charge your device wirelessly through microwave frequencies. In short, via Wave, you could simply stick your phone in your microwave to charge the battery. This sounds like a dream come true for many Apple users with drained batteries, but the service didn't really exist.

Food giant Campbell went through a similar experience when an online prankster set up a fake Twitter account for the company's Pace Picante sauces and ended up in a crude and often hilarious online exchange with comedian Kyle Kinane. Kinane, thinking he was actually dealing with the official Pace social marketing team, ended up repeatedly mocking the brand on Twitter, only to have every one of his tweets, including some praising Pace's competitors, seemingly favorited by the brand.

For example, Kinane tweeted "Pace Picante-brand salsa officially endorses @MrsRenfros salsa as the tastiest super market salsa ever." Sure enough, the tweet was favorited by Pace. Kinane next tweeted: "@Pace_Foods only eats Tostitos salsa at the company Xmas party." Once again, another Pace favorite. Over the course of the day Kinane's tweets and Pace's "responses" continued until finally someone at Campbell realized they were a victim of a sophiscated joke involving a fake Pace Twitter account. The Campbell marketing team promptly notified everyone on Twitter that Pace Picante Sauces actually had no official Twitter account; thus, the entire thing was an elaborate hoax actually set up by one of Kinane's fellow comedians. To Campbell's credit, the company picked up on the hoax within 24 hours, thus avoiding an enduring #BaldforBieber social fiasco.

What marketers can learn from these examples is that data can flow just as quickly about a brand and its real or imagined products and services as it does about Justin Bieber. And as in Justin Bieber's case, this speed is not always positive. Whether inaccurate or accidental, false or misleading information can make its way around the Internet in the blink of an eye. Alternatively, positive information, including strong consumer word-of-mouth or brilliant creative advertising, can also swiftly spread through digital channels. The speed of data is a double-edged sword with both positive opportunities and negative consequences for marketers. It should not be ignored.

If You Rob a Bank, Turn Your Phone Off

Beyond size and speed, data is also becoming much smarter. Thanks to the Internet, and in particular to mobile devices, we now have a layer of intelligence in data that did not exist before.

Some of this intelligence is simply due to how the Internet is coded. It's what the geeks among us would call "metadata," which is information that is built into the code to provide an explanation of what the content is all about, kind of like an invisible *TV Guide* for the Internet. The Internet is full of this invisible metadata, which feeds into various algorithms and allows all sorts of clever things to happen. For example, metadata is the backbone of Google's search results or at least one of the most important elements. It is metadata that helps explain to Google's crawlers what that web page is all about and why it should be ranked as it is in a particular keyword search.

Cookies are another repository of metadata; in this case and depending on the scenario, they provide either personalized or anonymized information. Cookies are essentially files that reside on your PC, laptop, and mobile device and keep information about you. Companies use this data to deliver a smarter, more customized, sometimes even personalized Internet experience, whether it's your Amazon shopping experience or your personalized Yahoo home page. Later on in this book we will delve further into the wonderful world of cookies and how they can support your adaptive marketing efforts

Arguably the greatest contributor to intelligence in data is coming from the aforementioned surge in Internet usage via mobile phones and in particular from one critical piece of data: your location. People can now give permission to their carrier, operating system, or certain applications to geolocate their exact physical position in the real world. Such additional intelligence in data enables organizations to do all sorts of things.

For example, take the United States Marshals Service. For those unfamiliar with this illustrious force, the federal marshals are responsible for pursuing and arresting criminals across state borders, among other things. Created by George Washington, this service is the second oldest federal law enforcement agency, just behind the less glamorous but no less important United States Postal Inspection Service.

For many years it has taken the federal marshals an average of 42 days to find fugitive criminals. In short, historically it has been a rather long and laborious process, as represented in the four seasons and 120 episodes it took the lead character in the 1960s television series *The Fugitive,* Deputy Samuel Gerard, to track down his fugitive, Dr. Richard Kimble.

Today's federal marshals use data, particularly smart mobile data, to accelerate the tracking down of criminals. Take Felix and Luis Soto. In 2009, the Soto brothers robbed the Webster Bank in Berlin, Connecticut. The brothers managed to run away with a small fortune and quickly left Connecticut before the police arrived. Unfortunately for Felix and Luis, they had left their mobile phones on at the time of the bank robbery. As part of standard procedure now, federal marshals contact local telephone carriers to request records of what phones were active in a particular cell tower area on the day and at the exact time of the crime. In fact, major US mobile carriers now regularly receive millions of such requests.

Sure enough, Felix Soto was one of 169 mobile phone users in the vicinity at the exact time of the robbery. A quick review of criminal records put Felix's name on top of the suspect list, and within a very short period he was tracked down and arrested.

As a result of using smart mobile data, the average time it takes a federal marshal to find a fugitive from the law has dropped from 42 days to 2 days. If only *The Fugitive's* Deputy Samuel Gerard had had mobile data, that famous fictional TV series may have lasted two hours rather than four years. Moreover, he would have known much faster that Dr. Kimble was actually innocent.

Less Archery, More Ping Pong

Due to digital innovations, data has increased in size and in speed, and it is packed with more intelligence. It's also no longer a one-way street. In fact, data is more synchronous than ever before, with information constantly flowing back and forth in many different shapes and sizes.

Think of it in sports terms. In the analog marketing world, we generally took a similar approach to archery. Much like sending an arrow to a target's bull's-eye, we'd take a message and fire it a target audience and hoped it would hit the right spot. We'd then take another arrow out of the quiver and once again take another shot, never entirely certain if we'd hit the bull's-eye.

These days marketing is much closer to table tennis. Like a ping pong ball, data and dialogue go back and forth, often at a rapid pace, constantly adapting as conditions change. In our hyperconnected world, marketing can be a two-way discussion full of implicit or explicit data streams. Implicit data streams consist of information exchanged without the user doing much of anything, like Internet cookies, for example, which provide behavioral data as mentioned earlier. Explicit data is data a consumer chooses to provide, such as Facebook posts, e-mails, or tweets. Both data sets are essential to marketers.

This synchronous data flow can happen across devices, among numerous parties, in both implicit and explicit forms, and between the real and virtual worlds. Consider, for example, the Satellite Sentinel Project (SSP), which is using real-time synchronous satellite images to help combat genocide in Sudan. Before splitting into two countries, the Sudan People's Liberation Army, led by Sudanese President Omar al-Bashir, had repeatedly attacked the indigenous tribes of Darfur in an attempt at an ethnic cleansing of the area to keep Sudan from splitting apart. George Clooney partnered with John Prendergast, a former staffer at the US State Department, to start the SSP initiative. Clooney's idea was a simple one: if paparazzi and journalists can use new technologies and data to track him down and take photos, why can't the same technology be used to put a spotlight on the activities of the world's worst dictators?

Clooney and Prendergast contacted Digital Globe, which operates sophisticated satellite systems that orbit the Earth up to 45 times a day. These satellites take high-resolution images of over nearly 1 million square miles, and the images are refreshed every three hours. SSP used this smart data to identify unusual military movements in southern Sudan and then warned local citizens to evacuate cities that might face imminent attack by President al-Bashir and his henchmen. These warnings were often spread via social networks or other less digitalized forms of communication.

The SSP initiative is a classic example of using implicit and explicit synchronized data to create an ongoing loop of information that cuts across the virtual and physical worlds.

Secure?

There is a fifth and final factor of data that is worth discussing, namely, security, arguably one of the biggest topics currently facing the marketing industry and unfortunately one that is only going to become more important as we get more data. Marketers face a major challenge in the future to find the right and ethical balance between using data and also protecting consumers who are often unknowingly creating a trail of unsecured digital data exhaust.

Don't take my word for it, just consider this: according to *Consumer Reports*, over 50 percent of Facebook users engage in risky behavior on the social network.[13] A recent AOL survey found that 84 percent of people say they have never given away personal information online, but in reality 89 percent of have done so.[14] A further analysis from the United Kingdom's OCFOM (Office of Communications) discovered that 60 percent of people have lost control of their data.[15] Microsoft research found 84 percent of people in the United Kingdom are concerned about online privacy, and 30 percent of people are very concerned. However, when these same people were asked what they were doing about protecting their privacy, 49 percent said they were not doing anything at all.[16]

All of this research points to a common and increasingly important theme: while people understand the need to secure their data, many either chose not to do so or unwittingly are doing things that lead to potential problems. A long-standing industry myth has it that when consumers go online, they lower their normal behavior and their inhibitions to the same extent they would after drinking two glasses of wine. Internet psychologist John Suler has written extensively about people and how their online behavior becomes "disinhibited." In effect, people feel they can't be identified in the virtual world in the same way they can in the physical world. In essence, they believe they become invisible and anonymous.

Marketers must navigate through this increasingly complex world of privacy protection, knowing that even when they follow the industry's self-regulation guidelines, they may still come across some consumers who are simply doing dumb things that marketers shouldn't take advantage of or exploit even if this is, strictly speaking, legal.

Of course, data security is not a new topic for most companies; it's just that the problem continues to grow despite all of the collective learning. As far back as 2012, IBM reported more than 1,500 instances of companies losing personally identifiable information due to theft, inadvertent exposure, or basic negligence. Three years later, not much has really changed; indeed, the situation has possibly even gotten worse as more companies migrate their data to cloud-based solutions without proper security protocols in place. To make matters even worse, customers know about the problem. A recent HyTrust poll revealed that 73 percent of respondents believe that their personal and financial information shared and stored with companies is *not* safe.[17] High-profile hackings, such as the 2014 Sony "Guardians of Peace" debacle and retailer Target's massive data breach, don't build public confidence. The IDC reports that fewer than 20 percent of the world's data is actually protected.[18] As an adaptive marketer, your job should be clear: to take every measure you can to make sure your company's data is part of that 20 percent that is safe from hacking and other threats.

As you can see there is more to data than just its size. In a hyperconnected world, data is increasingly swift, synchronous, smart, and hopefully secure (see Figure 1.4).

Adapt or Die

Jack Welch once famously said: "There are only two sources of competitive advantage: the ability to learn more about our customers faster

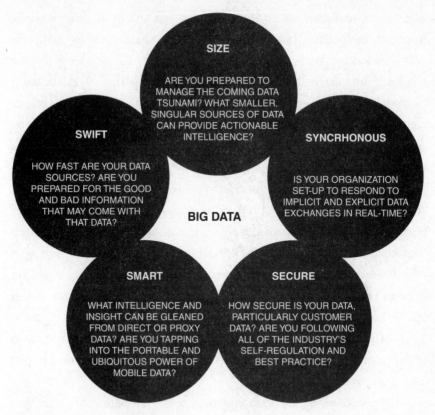

Figure 1.4 The Five S-Factors of Data.

than the competition and the ability to turn that learning into action faster than the competition."[19]

Little did General Electric's CEO know when he first made that simple but powerful statement that his company and many others would have such a wealth of data at their fingertips. More important, there is not only a vast amount of data available, but the other S-factors—swift, smart, synchronous, and secure—all add up to an incredibly powerful means for companies to know more about their customers than ever before. Companies can also act on that data faster than would have been imaginable when Jack Welch was CEO. All aspects of marketing, from advertising to product development, can be influenced and improved to make marketing more relevant to customers and more profitable to businesses.

As a consequence, according to those US marketers surveyed by Adobe in early 2014, big data ranks as their second highest concern, even outranking such high-profile media topics as social media and mobile.[20] Interestingly, it was the marketers with the largest budgets who found data to be more important rather than those from smaller companies. And there is a good reason for this: it's startling how many large companies, perceived as invincible, have failed to take Jack Welch's advice and have simply disappeared.

Take Borders, the chain founded in 1971 and conceived as a revolutionary new approach to book retailing. Borders and its competitor Barnes and Nobile grew to dominate the book industry, taking up a combined 40 percent of the book selling market by the 1990s. Those were heady days for the Borders management team, and the managers decided to rapidly expand the company's physical footprint not just in the United States but overseas in markets such as the United Kingdom. This wasn't just a physical expansion. Borders also jumped with both feet into the CD and DVD markets, effectively moving beyond books into music and films.

If the people on Borders management team had paid more attention to the data, they might have picked up on some compelling information that would have given them some of that gold-dust of customer learning that Jack Welch so famously praised. For while Borders was aggressively pursuing expansion, consumers were beginning to explore cheaper and simpler ways of buying entertainment, first by purchasing online via stores like Amazon and then by migrating to digital online platforms, like the Kindle for books or Apple's iTunes for music and film. It didn't help that Borders decided in 2001 to let Amazon control its online business. As a consequence, Borders failed to build up an independent online presence until 2008, thus completely missing an opportunity to build a loyal Internet customer base just as online sales boomed.

As a result, in little over ten years Borders's sales per square foot plummeted by nearly 34 percent from $261 in 1997 to $173 in 2009. By February 2011, the 40-year-old Borders chain had filed for bankruptcy with $1.29 billion in debt and $1.27 billion in assets. By the end of 2011, any hopes for a resurrection of Borders were dashed when the final 31 stores across 18 states were closed. The revolution in book retailing started by Tom and Louis Borders in Ann Arbor, Michigan, abruptly came to an end as other pioneering companies came along with adapted solutions for customers who had already adapted their behavior by moving their book purchasing preferences online.

Borders is only one example of the many companies that have gone out of business over the past twenty years as the Internet has provided the means for many new companies to disrupt previously impregnable industries and markets.

Kodak has arguably become the poster child of companies that failed to adapt to changing times. Despite inventing much of today's digital photography technology, during the late 1990s the company was way too slow in weaning itself off physical film. As a result, Kodak made its last profit in 2007 and ended up filing for Chapter 11 bankruptcy in early 2012. The Kodak corporation that remains today is a shadow of its former self, having been forced to sell most of its patents to new rivals such as Apple and Amazon and having stripped its business down to "personalized imaging and document imaging."[21]

Like so many similar stories, the key learning from both the Borders and the Kodak case is that regardless of a company's assets—history, size, distribution, brand equity—big companies can still disappear if they fail to understand their customers and adapt their businesses to reflect the new reality. According to Richard Foster, a professor at Yale, "by 2020, more than three-quarters of the S&P 500 will be companies that we have not heard of yet. The average life span of an S&P 500 company has decreased by more than 50 years in the last century, from 67 years in the 1920s to just 15 years today."[22]

For many marketers, Foster's prediction is a blunt wake-up call. Like Borders and Kodak and many others, if you fail to adapt to the times, particularly to customers and their ever-changing behavior and needs, you will go out of business. Fortunately, thanks to data, particularly real-time data from digital sources, you have more information and insight than ever before. Disappointingly, many companies aren't using this data. According to the IDC, less than 1 percent of the world's data is actually analyzed.[23]

The playing field has significantly evened out, and the old obstacles to new competitors and industry entrants have largely disappeared. Now more than ever you need to follow Jack's advice. Now more than ever you have the means to learn about your customers and to act and adapt your marketing based on that insight. You just need to do it faster than your competitors, both existing ones and those currently still sitting in a garage hatching plans to make you bankrupt. It's time to adapt or die.

CHAPTER 1.1

The Storyteller on DataGetting Past the Creepiness Factor

By Jeffrey Cole

Director, Center for the Digital Future, USC Annenberg
School for Communication

The term "big data" is joining "convergence," "synergy," and "information superhighway" as one of the most overhyped and least understood terms of the digital era. The problem is that we hear these terms constantly before they become part of our lives, and when they do, we are tired of their overuse and unsure about what they actually mean. Dan Ariely understood this problem about big data when he famously declared: "Big data is like teenage sex: everyone talks about it, nobody really knows how to do it, everyone thinks everyone else is doing it, so everyone claims they are doing it."[24]

"Big data" is real. We are collecting so much digital information on users, demographics, transactions, and much, much more that it is changing marketing in a way only George Orwell may have imagined several generations ago. Companies are afraid they are being left behind in understanding and using data. Those people who can patch together convincing data skills and experience are finding lucrative work as chief data officers, a title that did not exist a few years ago.

The problem with big data is that everyone is preoccupied with collecting data and few know the important questions to ask of their data. Without asking the right questions, databases are simply that: accumulations of big amounts of data.

Data can change everything. It can provide insights and understandings that were never before imagined. Applied to marketing, data can identify the 50 percent of John Wannamaker's advertising budget that was wasted. And used with problem controls, data can help consumers understand what they need and how to find it.

None of these important things can occur until we get past the "creepiness" factor. The creepiness factor kicks in when we realize that our innermost actions and thoughts are being watched and collected by someone else. It's sobering when even just looking at things online, perhaps out of curiosity and without serious intent, can be accumulated and "used against us." We are faced with being closely watched and perhaps judged.

The first time we realize big data are being used to market to us feels "creepy." Only once we understand what is actually happening and that we may greatly benefit from the use of our data does the creepiness begin to go away.

I clearly remember 25 years ago when I called American Express and a rep answered, "Hello, Mr. Cole, how may we help you?" It was disconcerting, and I looked around my house for cameras or some other way they could have known who I was. Once I understood the mechanics of caller ID, I no longer found such calls creepy and began to think of the use of my name as a courtesy. The now-classic case cited in *The Power of Habit* of Target determining from a teenage girl's online purchases that she was pregnant and sending her coupons for prenatal goods also raised creepiness to new levels.[25] The first time we are in a market and our mobile phones text us with coupons for the aisle we are stanwding in (and our shopping history on that aisle), we may want to turn off our phones forever and start paying only in cash. When we realize those coupons are for the items we need and that they offer substantial discounts, then the experience may no longer feel creepy. As long as we know what is being done with that data, we may welcome big data and our lives intermingling.

If we can get past the creepiness factor, then an unlimited wealth of possibilities exists in marketing. There is a clear benefit for marketers who, armed with high-quality data, can target their ads and offers toward people who need them and are much more likely to respond. They can eliminate the expense of paying to reach customers uninterested in their products. And this use of big data is a big win for consumers because they receive marketing that is useful and relevant rather than irrelevant and intrusive.

The era of big data in advertising is exciting and scary. The scariness can be contained when marketers follow four rules:

1. Marketers must tell consumers what information is being collected and what will be done with it.
2. There must be privacy statements not written by lawyers for lawyers. The statements may be written by lawyers, but they must be clear and simple to understand. For example, Steve Jobs admitted that he never read Apple's own privacy agreement because it was too complex.
3. There must be an easy way to opt in or opt out, and those who opt out must realize that they may have to pay more for items or services.
4. Consumers who opt in must be compensated, either in the form of cash or in the form of points, coupons, advance notice of sales, special events, or more.

In a world of big data marketing there will always be surprises, some of them unpleasant. But once we get past the creepiness factor and have some rules in place, few people will want to revert to an era where they received hundreds of unwanted, irrelevant messages.

CHAPTER 2

The World's Largest Focus Group

Once Upon a Time in Ohio

If you were growing up in Ohio in the 1970s before the Internet and cable TV, you had to make your own fun, whether it was building forts, setting up lemonade stands, or playing ding-dong-ditch. For my friends and me, one of our best sources of fun was going to the local Burger King and mixing together various soft drinks. A little Sprite combined with some Coca-Cola with a dash of Barq's Root Beer. Naturally we'd give the drink a name, like "Thunderball" or "Suicide," and we'd dare our friends to take a drink and keep it down. Often the drink would taste awful, but sometimes we'd stumble upon a magical combination, an elixir so good there was less daring and a lot more drinking. In effect, we were creating our own adaptive product, using our small group of good friends as a focus group, sampling each mixture to identify the good and bad. If only the Coca-Cola marketing research team could have eavesdropped on these little experiments at the Burger King soda fountain, some of our more popular variants might have actually made it beyond our small town in Ohio. Well, now Coca-Cola can do just that.

The Coca-Cola Freestyle vending machine takes that simple concept, which was most likely common in every town and village, and incorporates it in an actual vending machine. Freestyle vending machines now enable my kids to create their own special drinks by mixing together over 100 different Coca-Cola beverages. Just like me in my childhood, they can now use a vending machine to mix up Sprite, Coca-Cola, Barq's or any of the other 122 Coca-Cola beverages and variants, but there are a few special differences this time.

Freestyle vending machines are IP-enabled, which means that they are connected to the Internet; this allows you to not only mix your own drink and give it a name, but also to save it and share it with your friends via a mobile application. Rather than daring six buddies at Burger King to drink "Thunderball," you can now challenge the 150 or so friends you have on Facebook to sample your new beverage. Upon returning to the Freestyle machine, you and your buddies can simply use the Freestyle app to instantly recreate your special Coke concoction.

More important, Coca-Cola can now listen to and monitor all of these conversations and combinations that used to physically happen in a restaurant but now flow across the Internet. In effect, Coca-Cola has its very own real-time lab that provides its marketing team with instant data on what combinations and flavors are most popular with certain audiences. This vast amount of information and insight is being fed into the company's product development, which identifies trends and adapts not only the vending machine experience, but also new and variant products formally introduced into retail such as Fanta Cherry, which was a trending mix with Freestyle vending machine customers.

The business logic behind the new Freestyle machines is simple: faced with declining soft-drink sales, Coca-Cola needed to give today's millennials a reason to start drinking its products again, particularly in restaurants, an important part of the company's business. Coca-Cola's answer was to give millennials the ability to create their own products and then let them share the experience and their drinks via social networks such as Facebook and Twitter to build up the drinks' popularity.

Coca-Cola won't reveal the total investment it has made in Freestyle vending machines, but given the machines' importance to the future of the company's chunk of the $76 billion soft-drink business, one could assume it's a substantial investment. Freestyle machines are currently leased for $300 per month to restaurants and businesses; according to industry speculation, this amounts to approximately 60 percent more than a standard Coca-Cola fountain. However, according to Coca-Cola's research, nearly two out of three people say access to Coca-Cola Freestyle influences their choice of restaurant; remember Coca-Cola's Freestyle mobile app conveniently tells you what restaurants in your exact location have the machines. According to Jennifer Mann, Coca-Cola's vice president and general manager of Freestyle, all the company's data points to a significant uptick in business when the vending machines are installed. "We've proven prelaunch and in-market that when a restaurant has Coca-Cola Freestyle, their traffic, incidence and beverage servings grow anywhere from single to double digits," says Mann.[1] Apparently many businesses agree; at last count, Coca-Cola had expanded its Freestyle machines to more than 20,000 dispensers in the United States and United Kingdom, including Burger King restaurants.

The Coca-Cola Freestyle vending machine is just one example of how companies are using real-time data to enhance and improve their products, services, and experiences. Tapping into this rich stream of Internet data provides not just Coca-Cola, but any company that tries it, with arguably the world's largest focus group, a continuous virtual lab that can help marketers shape their product strategy to better meet consumer needs and to get one step ahead of the competition.

In fact, there is an entire spectrum of adaptive product approaches, ranging from a listening strategy to actual real-time adaptation, such as in the Coca-Cola Freestyle example.

Are You Listening?

Every day there are millions of conversations happening on the Internet, many of them about brands and products. The volume and depth of these conversations varies by category and by particular moments in time; Oreos may not normally be a major online topic unless the brand is advertising during the Superbowl and the lights happen to go out. Oreo's "You Can Still Dunk in the Dark" 2013 tweet was retweeted 10,000 times in just one hour. Clearly, there is a constantly fluctuating, volatile stream of chatter coursing through sites like Facebook and Twitter.

Some of this chatter is explicitly related to a brand and often requires some sort of response. The countless fan posts and follower tweets—positive, negative, and indifferent—should all ideally be managed and monitored. Recent research by GlobalWebIndex revealed that users are far more likely to interact with brands and brand content on Facebook than on either Twitter or Google+, with about one in four (23 percent) having clicked Like on a brand's Facebook page in the previous month; only 7 percent have followed a brand's Twitter profile, and a measly 6 percent have connected with the brand's Google+ page.[2] Nevertheless, according to Nielsen Social, there were 215 million tweets about brands in just the first quarter 2014 alone.[3] Extrapolate from that for the entire year, and you have nearly a billion tweets about brands, more than enough to deserve some notice from your marketing team.

While the numbers are informative, these statistics need constant reevaluation as these media platforms are continuously evolving their user experiences and algorithms—if they are not buying each other. These days many conversations don't even happen directly on Facebook or Twitter; instead, they happen in smaller communities or among friends, sometimes in user product reviews posted on Amazon, Travelocity, and other such forums. There's a whole lot of chatter going on in lots of different places online.

The good news is that there is technology available for companies to manage and monitor such discussions to extract valuable insight and information on brands and products and even on the competition. It is the integration of this information into the product development life cycle that is often lacking in many companies. Data often gets hoarded by a department and is not properly liberated under the right data protection protocols outlined later in this book. Companies, such as Kimberly-Clark, are beginning to extract such valuable data from these silos as they realize the full potential of such information throughout their business. Chris Whalen, Kimberly-Clark's Global Vice President of Integration, states, "The company has moved from how we are consuming data to now how do we parse it to the right people to get it quickly actioned."[4]

There are multiple listening tools on the market, and they change regularly as the technology evolves or, more often, as companies get acquired. Salesforce.com has been one of the major buyers of technology in this area for some time and has purchased the leading social monitoring tool Radian6 back in 2011 for $326 million. That particular acquisition has paid off as part of Salesforce's broader effort to build a more holistic adaptive marketing suite of cloud-based tools, which we will explore later. In the meantime, if you are just looking for a stand-alone social listening solution, here are a few tips from some of the world's biggest marketers.

Pay careful attention to this guidance. Implementing a social monitoring tool is a time-intensive process, particularly when done at an enterprise level. Assess and select wisely as there are many pros and cons and nuances that can come back to haunt you if not considered carefully. For example, many companies rush into selecting a tool for their market in the United States or the United Kingdom only to discover that the chosen solution has rudimentary to zero capability in languages other than English. Furthermore, to be truly beneficial for brands a listening tool needs to have some intelligence rather than just take comments at face value. For example, just reporting that "Dyson sucks" and categorizing that as negative sentiment may miss the point being made in natural language. "Dyson sucks" may be a concatenated positive comment given the company makes vacuum cleaners, which indeed suck things up really well.

Some of the leading tools in the market today include the aforementioned Salesforce.com's Radian6, which has the added benefit of increased integration into the company's overall technology stack. Salesforce's competitor Brandwatch has full access to Twitter and Facebook and claims to cover over 27 different languages. Another solution, Visible Technologies was once funded and used by the CIA;

therefore, it can't be too bad and must work in a few languages. There are many more options out there, and given the pace of change in the industry through technological advancements or acquisitions, it's always a good idea to revisit these solutions as they evolve.

Common Evaluation Criteria for Listening Tools

1. With which social networks does the tool operate? Can it listen to and monitor dialogue on Facebook, Twitter, Instagram, and other major social networks?
2. How customizable are the reports? Can they provide intelligence on your competitors, geographic locations, and specific demographics? What is the frequency of these reports? How expensive is the tool when it comes to such customization?
3. Can other data sources be integrated to develop correlations and more sophisticated reporting models? How "open" is the tool?
4. Can the tool accurately interpret trends? How accurate is its identification and classification of negative and positive comments?
5. In how many languages does the tool effectively operate? Can it understand all characters in all languages? What direct support is provided to local teams?

Finding a House of Cards in a Haystack

Some companies do get listening right. Take, for example, Netflix, the online entertainment company that streamed over 24 billion hours of content in 2014 and takes up nearly a third of Internet broadband every night in the United States. Even with this success, Netflix is under intense pressure from a variety of competitors ranging from HBO Go to Amazon's Prime to Apple's iTunes. Early on, Netflix decided that to win it must compete on more than just pricing and access to a recognizable content library. To differentiate itself from the competition Netflix decided to develop a unique product proposition, only available to Netflix customers. Something so compelling that existing customers would become advocates and new customers would flock to its service rather than that of its rivals. The solution sounds easy in principle, but it's much harder in practice.

How to identify this killer product, that proverbial needle in the haystack? Netflix logically turned to its data, poring over viewing patterns to try and identify some common themes that could lead to a solution. In short, Netflix listened to its customers.

What Netflix discovered from its viewing figures was that people really like movies starring Kevin Spacey as well as films directed by David Fincher. Furthermore, it noticed viewers had discovered an old BBC thriller dating from 1990 called *House of Cards*. Putting this data together, Netflix felt confident enough to commission a modern series of *House of Cards* set in Washington, D.C., rather than in London. This new series naturally starred Kevin Spacey and was directed by David Fincher. Unusually, Netflix decided to make all 12 episodes of this new series available to its subscribers immediately rather than follow the old, tedious linear viewing model that introduces new episodes week by week. Consumers ended up binge-watching episodes, viewing one after another, and this generated massive spikes in online buzz and, of course, a second and third season of the now award-winning *House of Cards*. Even better, after the launch of *House of Cards,* over three million new customers joined the streaming service. Netflix has acquired millions of new subscribers around the globe for a grand total of 57.4 million subscribers by the end of 2014. With this expansion, the company's revenue rose to $1.48 billion in the fourth quarter of 2014, up from $1.17 billion in 2013.

Not surprisingly, Netflix continues to develop original programming, including the recent *Orange is the New Black,* by analyzing its customer data and identifying subjects, stories, actors, directors, and any other element of a film or TV series that its users find compelling. Such an analysis does not replace the creative development process, but simply informs the latter and, hopefully, gives it a much greater chance of success.

The Netflix example highlights the need to monitor your own data for insights to inform your product strategy. Other companies look at the much broader universe of real-time consumer data available on the Internet. For example, it's common for many technology companies to closely monitor the Information Technology (IT) community to identify hardware and software issues and needs that can be instantly resolved or at least addressed by the support team. With such competitive margins and rapid product cycles, quickly enhancing or fixing features is critical to gaining even a slight increase in market share. Even elusive Apple is rumored to monitor various Apple forums to flag product issues, such as poor battery lifetime, and to work quickly to release a new version of an existing product to improve and eliminate such issues.

A monitoring approach to adaptive product development is arguably the simplest option. This approach enables a company to quickly discover how consumers feel about its products without any explicit expectation from or guarantee to those consumers that it will do anything with that data. The approach is inexpensive, unobtrusive, and instant. However, like most technology, it requires some intelligent input and governance from people. Here are some tips to help your teams establish a great listening program.

Top Tips for Good Listening

1. Be clear about your objectives. Make sure to gain agreement internally on what information you are seeking from your social listening and monitoring and how that information will get distributed throughout your organization.
2. Carefully define what you are monitoring. Based on your objectives make sure you are defining exactly what you are monitoring. The tools are only as useful as the input you enter into them. Carefully define target audiences, competitors, and key topics and trends you want to follow.
3. You still require people to analyze the data. The reporting and diagnostics from the tools, particularly regarding sentiment, are powerful. However, you will still need analysts to review the information to identify nuances and determine the optimal actions to take.

4. Identify advocates and detractors. Use your sentiment data to identify powerful online advocates and detractors and develop a plan to leverage their influence to the benefit of your brand.

5. Develop rules and guidelines to act on the information. Don't let the data just sit in a report. Ensure the information and insight reaches the right people in your organization so they can take action to improve the business. In particular, be ready to respond to any major events, for example, product defaults, in real-time before they grow into larger issues.

Why Starbucks Has Molasses Cookies

Some companies have decided to take a step beyond monitoring by using the Internet to actively engage with consumers to identify new products or enhancements to existing ones. There are a variety of models and options available to marketers. For example, many brands have simply created basic Facebook brand pages and have extended an open invitation to people to post ideas.

Starbucks has been one of the pioneers in using consumer data to adapt its products and retail experience. It launched its My Starbucks Idea several years ago on Facebook, Twitter, and a few other online destinations.

The Starbuck's model is simple. Starbucks customers can submit an idea to the community. The community then comments and votes on these ideas. All of the ideas are tracked on a leaderboard, which also includes those customers who have been the most active in submitting ideas, leaving comments, and voting. Customers are even allowed to riff off the ideas of others, making additional suggestions to make the concept even more compelling and actionable. Ideas that make it past this initial filter are then evaluated by Starbucks, and some are deemed feasible while others are rejected with an explanation.

The program generated over 7,000 ideas from consumers in its first year, and at last count now has over 190,000 submissions since launch.[5] Hundreds of user-generated ideas have been embraced by the community and subsequently successfully implemented by Starbucks, including free coffee for Gold Card members on their birthday, the Starbucks VIP card, and molasses cookies. In addition, on average, three new products, concepts, or variations are tested somewhere every week due to an idea posted on My Starbucks Idea. And most important, customers love these ideas. More than 5.8 million cake pop treats are enjoyed each year thanks to Idea #128. As for Idea #1: the introduction of splash sticks, which have mercifully kept many Starbuck's customers clothes much cleaner over the years. Big or small, Starbucks welcomes any adaptive idea.

My Starbuck Ideas by Product to Date[6]

- 43,915 coffee and espresso drinks
- 5,787 Frappuccino® beverages
- 12,489 tea and other drinks
- 21,514 food
- 10,711 merchandise and music
- 22,499 Starbucks card
- 5,261 new technology
- 13,771 other product ideas

LEGO is another company that has long used online communities to source new product ideas. LEGO Ideas enables LEGO fanatics to submit ideas for new LEGO sets. The community votes on the ideas, and ideas getting over 10,000 votes formally move on to the LEGO Review stage, where the LEGO team evaluates the ideas to ensure they are safe, a good fit for the brand, and playable. If you are lucky enough to get your product idea manufactured, you even get a percentage of the sales.

The Lego Ideas site has been a hit, with nearly 600,000 users submitting over 60,000 projects to date; moreover, some 175,000 friendships have been created as LEGO fanatics follow each other's projects. According to LEGO sources, to date ten major products have been launched, including the phenomenally successful LEGO Architecture series, which has been a huge success for the company and now consists of over twenty buildings, all firmly established in the company's main product. *Back to the Future* and *Ghostbusters* kits are two of the other major products that have emerged from LEGO Ideas. What's greatly appealing about these user-generated concepts is that they mainly appeal to adults or what LEGO calls AFOLS (Adult Fans of Lego), a group willing and able to spend more money on LEGO than children do. LEGO is reluctant to share hard numbers behind the program, but its expansion coupled with the company's continued financial success must be some sign of management's confidence in the approach to product development.[7]

Other companies have created similar communities to get feedback and ideas on products and services. In some cases these are closed, invitation-only communities that serve two primary functions. The first is to capture insight and ideas from specific audiences and/or experts in a particular area. The second function is to build a strong group of vocal brand advocates; these are individuals who feel they have contributed to the brand experience and therefore have some sense of ownership of it.

But you don't necessarily need to build this on your own. There are companies that can specifically set up this type of product innovation and development. For example, sites like Quirky and Kickstarter enable individuals, mainly entrepreneurs, to submit their product ideas to an already existing community to have these concepts evaluated and, hopefully, get funding. Similar to My Starbucks Ideas, these communities then can vote on ideas and add more thoughts to it to make the idea more compelling and effective. Quirky will actually take over the product development process, including financing, prototyping, manufacturing, and ultimately selling the product online. In exchange for all of this, the product innovator must sign over all intellectual property (IP) rights to Quirky, but the entrepreneur retains a cut of the gross revenues. This is an interesting new business model, one with greater financial incentive for customers; it may inspire adaptive marketers in their quest to better tap into customers who may have great ideas related to a brand but no practical experience in implementing their ideas. Kickstarter, on the other hand, acts as more of crowd-funding platform for new product ideas rather than as a one-stop shop for outsourcing product development.

Similarly, P&G has also experimented with such outsourced, crowdsourcing models. The Oral-B marketing team launched an unbranded product innovation contest on the crowdsourcing platform eYeka to see what people would dream up when it comes to a connected toothbrush. Within 22 days, the eYeka community came up with 67 credible suggestions from 24 countries. While it won't replace P&G's $2 billion investment in research and development, the eYeka program does enable the company to tap into new sources of ideas coming directly from consumers.

While not for everyone, such outsourced, crowdsourcing models should certainly be understood if not explored; at a minimum, it's probably worth it to monitor what your next competitors are up to and check out their fledgling ideas. Places like Kickstarter may in fact be today's equivalent to the start-up garage of years past.

Top Tips for Good Engagement

1. Make sure you are committed. There is nothing worse than setting up a community with high expectations and then simply failing to live up to your promises. Your strongest advocates will very quickly become your strongest detractors.
2. Be clear on the rules and rewards. Lack of clarity can lead to disappointment and possibly future legal problems. Ensure people understand the process, the parameters, and ultimately the process of how decisions will be made.
3. Share the success. As ideas turn into real products and services, make sure you are sharing these success stories with the community to show its members that this is real and you are taking them seriously.
4. Be prepared for bad things. The more open your community, the higher the probability that you will attract troublemakers, particularly if you are in an industry that carries even the slightest whiff of controversy. Be prepared to manage your community in a professional manner. Whatever you do, don't take the bait.

5. Keep the connection active. Good engagement means you need to actually engage on a regular basis. Avoid the digital equivalent of tumbleweed in your community by regularly posting contests, special content, messages from management, etc., Encourage members of your community to engage with each other.

If You Can Do It with Goldfish and M&Ms

Of course, in today's digital world, companies can offer a greater degree of adaptability beyond just implicitly or explicitly sourcing ideas from consumers. One such way is to enable customers to customize products, either through some basic personalization or more detailed configuration.

For many marketers, offering some level of product adaptability is more than a gimmick, it's a critical requirement to maintain customer loyalty and build some margin in their business. Marketers are now faced with the most informed consumers in the history of mankind. Every teenager wielding a smartphone can get an instant price comparison, search product reviews, or find a cheaper alternative with a couple of swipes of the finger. According to Nielsen, 49 percent of mobile phone owners use their device to compare prices, frequently when in a physical store—a trend known as "showrooming."[8] For marketers instantly adaptable products are one path to building greater customer interest and loyalty to a brand, and they are also a means to get customers to spend some extra cash in the process.

The good news is that consumers seem to like the idea of adaptive products. A recent 2013 Bain[9] survey of more than 1,000 online shoppers in the United States found that while less than 10 percent have tried customization options, 25 percent to 30 percent are interested in doing so, a number bound to increase as e-commerce continues to expand. That very same Bain survey found that customers are also willing to pay up to 20 percent more for adaptive products, which will be welcome news to those marketers seeking some incremental margin. For example, according to Bain, if 25 percent of online sales of footwear were customized, the market would grow by $2 billion per year. Furthermore, the Bain research discovered that customers who designed their own shoes gave companies a 50 percent higher Net Promoter Score[SM] (NPS®), which is a standard way of measuring a customer's loyalty and usually equates to higher sales, advocacy, and lifetime customer value. This is one of many solid reasons why companies from Nike to Adidas offer some type of customizable shoes online.

A passion for adaptive products is also a generational trend. Today's young digital natives are accustomed to personalizing nearly everything, even toys, and to mass-customizing products. In fact, some of the hottest retailers cater to this so called "I Designed It Myself Effect," that allows shoppers to gain a sense of accomplishment from codesigning products, a behavioral trait reinforced and turbocharged through years of generating content and personalizing experiences on the Internet.

Arguably a perfect manifestation of this trend toward adaptive products is the ultimate girl's toy, a doll. My American Girl enables you to create your very own bespoke doll, not only changing physical features but also personality and character, as your doll is not only physically produced but also lives in a virtual world. According to the company, over 25 million American Girl dolls have been sold through the company's catalogue, retail stores, and website since 1986, and the company's catalogue is now the largest consumer toy catalogue and ranks as one of the top 30 consumer catalogues in the country. American Girl has developed a large and vocal online fan base, including numerous bloggers, and now gets over 72 million users a year to visit the American Girl website.

Sales of American Girl dolls increased by 20 percent from 2012 to 2013 and added $122.3 million to the bottom line for toymaker Mattel.[10] To put this in perspective, poor Barbie only went up by three per cent during the same period. The adaptive model behind American Girl explains a lot of this gap in performance. While a basic doll will set you back around $125, by the time you have purchased all the accessories, including shoes and hair extensions, you are looking at a hefty $300 price tag. The lesson: people are willing to pay more for customized products, sometimes a lot more.

You may argue that adapting dolls and other products isn't a new concept. You would be correct: customization and personalization have been around since the very early days of the Internet. Certain industries and companies, such as automotive and computer manufacturers, have made customization a core feature of their online sales process for years. Dell has long offered consumers the ability to configure their computer with dozens if not hundreds of different options. What has changed since the early days of the Internet is both the wider interest in customization in other product categories as well as the commercial feasibility for marketers to customize. In short, more consumers are interested in adapting certain products, and more companies can now profitability do it at scale.

Take, for example, Pepperidge Farm, the company that now lets customers personalize their Goldfish crackers at its My Way website. While the cracker still looks like a fish, customers can adapt the color, flavor, and even the packaging, adding a photo of their kids and a special message, for example. According to Pepperidge Farm's president, Irene Chang Britt, people are personalizing Goldfish crackers for all types of events ranging from weddings to graduations to proms. Britt cites the Goldfish My Way as a great example of innovation that attracts new customers, one of the three strategic growth drivers she sees behind the business.

My M&Ms is Goldfish My Way on steroids. The idea for My M&Ms originated with British ex-pat Neils Willocks, who moved to the United States in 2003 to join Mars company's Advanced Development Group. Willocks was fascinated with the all-American candy and in particular with the enthusiastic response from customers whenever a customized version was released for special events, such as Halloween and Valentine's Day. Willocks wondered whether this customization could be taken to another level, and was soon given an initial $250,000 research and development budget to experiment with technology and other means of adapting M&Ms. The challenge with this level of customization was how to do it at a low enough cost so that it could be profitably scaled and priced to appeal to customers used to paying next to nothing for their M&Ms. Eventually Willocks and his team discovered ink-jet technology that lowered order lead times down to hours and, more important dropped the $1,500 cost of each order to a price point acceptable to customers.

Eventually the website launched in 2004 with one production machine, and within hours it was swamped by orders for personalized and customized candy. Overwhelmed by the response, the company shut down the website and reopened it a week later after increasing capacity, and the company also raised the price based on that initial demand. Orders doubled immediately, indicating that people were willing to pay a higher price for customized products. Over the years Mars has increased the adaptability of the product. Consumers can not only choose the color and words on their M&Ms, they can also adapt the packaging, put an image on the candy, even logos from their favorite sports teams, maybe even Elvis. At this point, there is virtually nothing that can't be adapted when it comes to M&Ms, and this is one of the reasons the web site has become one of the most successful in the confectionary business.

Putting More Magic into the Magic Kingdom

Adaptive marketing principles are not limited to products. The service industry is also creating adaptive experiences based on real-time data.

I'm a big Disney fan. I've been to the Disney theme parks countless times and hope to go many more times in the future. Like many others, I have some personal favorites: Space Mountain, Pirates of the Caribbean, Haunted Mansion, for example, and even the Tikki Room gives me goose bumps.

There's really only one thing that annoys me at Disney: lines, sometimes really long lines. At least these days we have mobile phones to pass the time, but it's still downtime when there is so much to do and explore (and spend more money on).

Recognizing this small hiccup in customer experience, Disney has recently deployed a new technology called Magic Band at the Orlando theme park. Visitors to the Walt Disney World Magic Kingdom can register in advance of their trip at mydisneyexperience.com and create a custom experience including planning what rides they want to go on and when, thereby avoiding or at least minimizing waiting in those long lines. These visitors are then issued a Magic Band, which is a physical wristband with wireless NFC (near field communication) capability. The Magic Band keeps all this data, including the customer's profile, credit card, and customized theme park experience, and enables them to check in at rides at the times they specified as well as to buy food and gifts with one tap on the band. The wristband even acts as hotel room key; Disney had to change over 28,000 door locks just for Magic Band. In effect Magic Band is a theme park "fastpass" and a credit card in one device—the Mouse House's version of wearable technology. Visitors can even chose their own Magic Band color and add a name to the band.

What makes this initiative so special is that the Magic Band data flows both ways. The band tracks what you do in the park, the items you purchase, the characters you meet, and then adapts your ongoing online experience with Disney to make it more relevant. For example, if you spent a lot of time with Goofy at the theme park, Goofy will be the main character greeting you on the website after your visit. It's an adaptive and synchronized physical and virtual experience based on your interests and activities.

Rumored to have cost over $1 billion, Disney is trying out Magic Band only at its Walt Disney World theme park in Orlando, but it has big plans for expanding this technology to its other theme parks once it has been fully tested and embedded. In the end consumers get a highly personalized and hassle-free experience at the Magic Kingdom Park while Disney not only frees up more time visitors normally spend waiting in lines for rides, but with one tap enables them to charge all those food, drinks, and shopping costs to one online bill.

How is it working so far? Disney is coy about revealing too much data, particularly given that it's still early days, and the technology is still being stress-tested. However, what we do know is that over ten million Magic Bands have been handed out so far, wait times for park entry are down by 25 percent, and 75 percent of Magic Band users engage with the experience at MyMagic+. Walt would be proud.

To Adapt or Not to Adapt

We've presented many great case studies on how companies can leverage the Internet and real-time data to adapt their brands of products, services, and experiences: Netflix's data monitoring to identify new products, Starbuck's active engagement with consumers to solicit new ideas, Mars's use of online connections to adapt products and packaging, Disney creating an adaptive physical and virtual experience. These are all inspiring examples, but should every brand adapt its products and services based on input from consumers?

There are several factors to consider when contemplating an adaptive approach to products.

First, do your customers have an actual interest in adapting your product or service? What may seem like a good idea hatched in a marketing brainstorming session may in reality be perceived as a terrible one by your customers. For example, the Dutch airline KLM's Meet & Seat program lets you find out about interesting people who will be on board your KLM flight, such as other passengers attending the same event as you at your destination. It's an opt-in experience that uses a passenger's LinkedIn and Facebook data and shares that with other individuals on the same flight. Consequently, you can change your seat to get closer to a business colleague or prospect. The problem with Meet & Seat is that most airline travelers have no desire to have someone presenting a sales pitch to them during a flight.

According to KLM, more than 50,000 of the airline's 52 million annual passengers have chosen to use Meet & Seat since the service was introduced; this amounts to less than 1 percent. The reasons for poor customer adoption may have best been captured in an interview in *Mashable* magazine. Ben Hammersley, a frequent KLM traveler, dared to publically state what most business travelers privately think: they have no interest in doing business when on an airplane. In fact, flying remains one of the few downtime zones, where busy workers get a chance to disconnect and take a break. In the words of Hammersley: "You'd have to drown yourself in gin before the end of the flight.

In my job you just spend the entire time being pitched at or dealing with people who are constantly on. Planes are a refuge from that."[11] Hammersley also pointed out possible awkward social moments as colleagues reject seatmates or accidentally end up sitting next to someone they would rather avoid.

In other situations customers simply may have limited interest or time to adapt a product. This may be particularly true of low consideration mass products where people have less emotional interest in the customization, although Goldfish crackers and M&Ms have clearly put that theory to the test. In the end, the value exchange of a company investing incremental effort to make a product adaptable must be equivalent to the additional interest, time, and money required from consumers. Some solid foundational research should be able to answer this simple but fundamental question.

A second factor to consider is whether the economics make sense. While consumers may be interested in personalizing or configuring the product, the manufacturing and delivery process required may dilute the profit margin rather than add to it. In short, you'll lose money. As technology advances, particularly with the emergence of 3D printing, the costs of such adaptions will go down. In the meantime, a careful analysis of the cost-benefit ratio will help. Furthermore, the level of adaptability should be considered. There may be some simple customization features that meet most consumers' needs and constitute most of the incremental margin that can be captured. Use customer data and research to identify these mission-critical features instead of creating a multimillion dollar "all singing, all dancing" customization capability that is largely left unused by your customers. For example, consider a recent failure on the part of Estée Lauder; the company launched its Prescriptives brand with great fanfare only to see it subsequently discontinued because it failed to capture any interest from the youth market it targeted. Prescriptives, which was sold in department stores such as Nordstroms, offered women and young girls custom color matching services for skin-care products. In fact, at the time Estée Lauder's

Prescriptives was the only makeup brand that created foundations, powders, bronzers, and lip color on the spot at a customer's request by matching, blending, and rematching foundation colors—essentially offering adaptive cosmetics.

On the surface it sounds like a great idea. However, dig a bit deeper, and several serious flaws emerge. First, Prescriptives was a new brand that was unable to provide free samples and gifts due to the highly customized nature of the product; there were no mass-produced items to give away. Consequently, Prescriptives was unable to use proven marketing tactics that other brand builders had successfully used elsewhere. Furthermore, the Prescriptives brand's target audience proved to be more influenced by trending hot new colors than by a customized product. In effect, they wanted what everyone else wanted, not something unique to them. Finally, the price point ultimately led to an unprofitable business as the time required for a customized makeup process was a turnoff for time-starved consumers and meant huge labor costs for Estée Lauder. CEO Freda Fabrizio finally closed the entire affair down with a succinct statement: "After a thorough analysis of the Prescriptives brand, management concluded that the brand's long-term business model is no longer viable given the current market environment."[12]

Toyota Motor Company also had a similar adaptive failure when it attempted to create a mass customization model for automobiles at the same cost as that of standardized, mass-produced cars. Inevitably, production costs soared, inventory needs at dealerships multiplied, and the business turned unprofitable. An investigation by Toyota management revealed that 20 percent of the product varieties accounted for 80 percent of the sales; this was effectively the 80/20 model. The lesson here is that you can take adaptability to an extreme, and if there is not a solid business case to support such extensive adaptation, that is, customers willing to pay for it, it may have unintended consequences.

Finally, know your brand values and stick with them. Don't chase every product extension or adaptive opportunity. In fact, with some brands the less adaptive the product, the more appealing. Many luxury brands are attractive to consumers precisely because they can't be personalized or adapted. In fact, these brands and products are somewhat elusive, accessible only to those fortunate enough to buy them. Ironically, sometimes the less adaptive a product is, the more compelling it is. However, even in these scenarios there is still room for some adaptability. In these cases the adaptive component may lie in the experience and service that surrounds the actual product; effectively the highly personalized red-carpet treatment that accompanies the expensive watch, the fancy dress, the glamorous car, even the private bank account.

Top Tips for Good Customization

1. Make sure your customers are interested. A more advanced approach to adaptive products requires some robust research to ensure your customers actually care about customization. Run through some use cases to make sure you've thought through all the benefits and the issues.
2. Do the math. You may have some great ideas to enable mass customization, but they could also bankrupt you. Ensure your adaptive approach will actually add margin to the business and that your customers will be willing to pay for that extra customization.
3. Stay true to the brand. Your customers may like your product because it cannot be adapted. Some luxury products may benefit from adaptive service rather than from adapting the product.
4. Understand the business implications. Ensure that your business is committed to the change required for highly customized products and services, which can impact every part of the supply chain.
5. Outmaneuver the competition. Keep an eye on the traditional competition and the Kickstarters of the world to make sure whatever you develop is more compelling and potentially disruptive.

Our next chapter explores how brands are using real-time data to adapt and improve customer service. However, before moving on take a look at these three adaptive options to see whether your company is currently tapping into any of these opportunities to feed into what

	LISTEN	ENGAGE	CUSTOMIZE
APPROACH	Use social monitoring and listening tools to identify new adaptive opportunities.	Invite customers to provide specific ideas for new or enhanced products, services, and experiences. Use evaluation mechanisms (voting, experts, etc.) to assess and progress.	Enable customers to adapt the product, service, or experience in real-time, often via personalization and customization.
LEADERS	Netflix	Starbucks, LEGO	Coca-Cola, Disney, Dell
PRO'S	Low-cost and low-touch approach. Doesn't require any customer knowledge or engagement.	Open approach to encourage customers to provide ideas and suggestions, which in itself may build loyalty and advocacy. A private invitation only approach is also possible when wishing to get input from a specific set of customers.	If valued by the consumer, this approach offers the ultimate personalized experience with the brand. Can drive loyalty, advocacy, and most importantly margin.
CON'S	A passive approach that may miss opportunities and ideas that customers would suggest if given the opportunity.	Requires greater on-going commitment to manage the program. Marketers must also demonstrate that they are evaluating and acting on the suggestions.	Highly dependent on manufacturing and functional feasibility. Also must align with brand positioning and customer desires.

Figure 2.1　Different Adaptive Approaches for Products and Services.

P&G's Global Marketing Director Stephen Squire calls "the lifeblood of the business"[13] (see Figure 2.1). If you are part of the 69 percent of marketers cited by Dunnhumby as being greatly concerned about new product development, there may just be a an adaptive marketing approach that gets you and your company to a less stressful and more competitive place when it comes to new products and services.

CHAPTER 2.1

The Creative Agency on Data

Laurent Burman
Global Chief Client Officer at POSSIBLE

This obsession with data—it stifles creativity and risk taking. It sucks the emotion out of the the creative output and ideas. We should treat it with caution. It is a tool that's in danger of becoming a weapon.

You hear these types of statements all the time, even from some of our industry's foremost leaders. This posture makes for great onstage performances at Cannes and pithy sound bites in the trade media, and it (artificially) foments debate in marketing and advertising circles around the showdown between "big ideas" and "big data."

The statements above are entertaining, but they're not true— or at least they're not true for today's most successful companies, brands, or agencies. For these organizations, data is actually liberating and creates new opportunities in its own right. The key to unlocking the real power of data—which goes beyond a mere input that supports or determines the creative idea —is to adopt an adaptive marketing approach to it that uses what we know about the things we can measure to help create a satisfying human experience. That doesn't mean that we should evaluate or judge our work solely by quantitative measures that are too often inadequate to measure the full human and business impact of our work. There will always be important things that we simply can't measure—or can't measure precisely, easily, or inexpensively enough to be useful. Sometimes we have to "go with our gut"—based on imperfect or incomplete information or, better still, in spite of the data if we deem it to be inadequate. But it's our ability to mine and interpret the growing mountains of data generated by our actions, our communications, and even our devices that can both embolden and challenge us in our decisions. Data mining is not foolproof, but it's a better litmus test than we've ever had—and for those willing to make the leap, the ways of using data are only getting better.

At POSSIBLE, we find that a data-aware approach to our creative work combined with a culture comfortable with testing and learning (failing fast and cheaply, if you will) makes us more agile and adaptive in the face of changing realities; it frees us to take more risks. It also enables us to make important decisions more quickly and with greater confidence. Our success depends on a harmonious relationship between intuition and data—big data *and* big ideas, if you will.

Our approach to data, which includes modeling where direct measures elude us, frees us up to spend our time creating work that we're passionate about and that is effective and impactful. We've reorganized our structure so we can collaborate differently, tearing down the traditional walls between media, marketing sciences (data/analytics), creative, and strategy in favor of a shoulder-to-shoulder approach of working together to generate more insights and, consequently, much richer, more nimble, and more compelling creative solutions.

In short, our creative teams embrace data and can speak knowledgeably about it, and the people on our analytics team are always thinking about how their findings can fuel insights, vet ideas—and create and expand on them as well. The result? Smart, resonant creative solutions that work beautifully.

Let's look at two famous examples of data-aware companies and at what we can learn from them.

Netflix and Amazon are staunchly data-driven organizations that are leveraging their data prowess to disrupt, among other things, the motion picture and television industries. When Netflix in early 2013 plunked down $100 million for two seasons of *House of Cards* and beat out all the other networks—including industry visionaries such as HBO and ShowTime—most people were shocked and more than a little dismissive. But after launch (to critical acclaim and audience traction), it became clear that Netflix knew something others didn't. And the company knew it because it had gathered a vast trove of data. Netflix knew about users and their viewing habits and preferences; in addition, where available data was too imprecise to be useful, it created vast new data sets to categorize content in far more granular and useful ways than had been possible previously. This allowed Netflix to recognize the strong correlation between the *House of Cards* project and the interests of a specific but substantial potential audience that intuition alone had seemingly missed. The data helped the company act with confidence—even though the final outcome, as in any creative endeavor, was, of course, anything but certain.

One of the company's more recent endeavors, *Marco Polo*, was largely panned by critics and the cognoscenti alike when it launched in December 2014. And yet, despite the dismal reviews, it has an average rating of 8.3 on IMDb and 4.3 out of 5 on Netflix, with over 1.2 million reviews—and counting. The people at Netflix apparently clearly understand what their audience will respond to and cater to that—despite what critics make of it all.

Amazon also has a massive collection of data about the content that people buy and—having acquired IMDb in 1998—it also knows what movies and shows people like. Lacking the same volume of streaming information (Netflix's streaming marketing share is roughly 57 percent, and Amazon's is 3 percent) and the detailed categorization data Netflix had, Amazon took a very different tack. The people at Amazon chose to garner and mine vast amounts of consumer feedback to help them decide which pilots to green-light and which of these to fund for a full series. This approach gives Amazon the creative freedom to try more initiatives cheaply and quickly—allowing content creators to get and give feedback and audiences to be vested in what succeeds—and Amazon can then invest more heavily and with greater confidence in those projects that are proving successful.

As Amazon's vice president of content will attest, it's not as if a computer or a panel is making the decisions, but the company is getting the signals and validation needed to make informed business decisions about bold, new, creative ideas. The critical success of the Amazon Studios 2014 release of *Transparent*, which won a Golden Globe Award for Best Television Series, suggests that Amazon is on a right track.

"*A* right track," not "*the* right track." One of the biggest lessons we have to learn in this data-saturated age is that data isn't one fixed thing with a definite use and purpose. Data comes in many forms, and there are many ways to use it, many things to measure, many insights to be derived from what we learn, many ways to adapt to what we are learning. A data-aware and adaptive marketing mind-set allows agencies and companies to do four important things better than they've ever been done before:

1. **Generate better insights.** Teams can leverage modern tools and techniques to combine vast, previously disparate data sets and make sense of them quickly. Starbucks, for example, hit one out of the park with its #sipface campaign, which recognized that Frappuccino drinkers focus enthusiastically on life's little joys. This hugely successful social

media campaign sprang from information revealed by deep analysis of consumer behavior and was validated through rapid testing.

2. **Learn and grow (faster).** Failing fast (and cheaply) can be OK and may even be necessary in order to test hypotheses and explore boundaries. Having data scientists, strategists, and creatives collaborating to understand not just what worked and what didn't—but for whom, when, where, and even why—builds trust and accelerates learning. As part of our work for Ford, the creative team developed what it thought was really effective video—but at an expense that traditional traffic and engagement key performance indicators (KPIs) didn't justify. Qualitative data, however, suggested that select and important audiences loved the video. Our data science team built models to understand what might be depressing the metrics as well as prove the creative team's hypothesis. We found that, in fact, these videos were having a huge impact on test-drives (a useful proxy that had been correlated to sales). In the end, the client tripled the video budget, and the business and the brand grew as a result.

3. **Make bigger, bolder bets.** Teams can help protect their best, but potentially riskier, ideas from being dismissed or otherwise watered down through the inevitable process of self-censorship, internal or client reviews, or "approvals" from important and even well-meaning stakeholders who might not be the best equipped to evaluate the work and are deciding based on their gut feelings.

4. **Attract great talent.** A dynamic, inquisitive, fearless environment sets up exceptional creatives to be more exceptional. Kevin Spacey jumped at *House of Cards* for Netflix because the company's data made it confident enough to give him two years of creative freedom—no pilots, no tests.

Being data-aware can ultimately drive the best creative talent right to your door.

We've now entered an age when marketing agencies and creative teams won't be treating data merely as a tool—instead, data is becoming a catalyst for wholesale transformation of the workplace, changing how creative ideas are generated, executed, and adapted to achieve their intended purpose. Instead of big data competing against big ideas, the relationship looks more like this: Useful Data + Great Creative + Agility = Big Ideas That Work.

CHAPTER 3

#HappyCustomers

I n the preceding chapter we looked at how marketers are leveraging data, particularly fast-moving online data, to adapt their products and services, whether instantly adaptable Coke products or crowdsourced product idea generation. All of this adaptation is feasible due to the rise of synchronous, fast-moving digital data and technology. In addition to great product ideas, this fast-moving data may also include some other vital information that needs a much quicker response from the brand. In some cases this data may convey a crisis, in other cases it's just a straightforward customer service need. Regardless, in today's hyperconnected world, people expect brands to respond and to respond quickly.

The Kryptonite Incident

It all started with Kryptonite—not the stuff that takes down the mighty Superman, but the bike lock brand.

It was 2004 when Chester Bullock decided to put an urban legend to test by using a simple Bic pen to pick and unlock the supposedly impregnable Evolution 2000 bicycle lock. To his shock, it actually worked. The lock was unlocked. The impossible was possible.

Chester duly videotaped the entire process and notified the good folks at Kryptonite that they had a serious problem at hand. The highly marketed all-star product was actually a dud; any bicycle thief with a cheap ballpoint pen could snatch someone's bike in seconds.

Kryptonite eventually responded with a short explanation on the historical benefits of tubular cylinders, which was as fascinating as it sounds. The company even had the gall to use the occasion to promote its new disc cylinder products. In short, it did nothing other than send Chester some recognition of having received the e-mail. Like Superman's Kryptonite, the incident put the company into some sort of unearthly mental deep freeze.

Meanwhile, Chester posted his short "How To Unlock a Kryptonite Lock With a Bic Pen" video on YouTube, and eventually people started to notice and share it with their friends. Within a month the original posted video was viewed thousands of times, not to mention shared around the web, and then the story got picked up by the mainstream press. Kryptonite products were pulled from the shelves of thousands of bike retailers, and sales plummeted. In addition, thousands of customers now had a legitimate claim to Kryptonite's product insurance policies, which promised reimbursements of up to $3,000 to replace any bike stolen that had been secured, or in reality not so secured, with one of its locks. In the words of Chester's notorious video, the Kryptonite Lock was hereby technically considered a "piece of crap."

In the end, the Kryptonite lock incident became one the Internet's legendary failures, and arguably woke up an entire generation of marketers to the threats and opportunities the Internet brings when it comes to customer service and a brand's reputation. Rather than burying their heads in the sand, marketers suddenly realized that the Internet could swiftly damage, even destroy, their business in a short period of time. Alternatively, the Internet could also be a remarkable tool that could be used to rapidly adapt and spread communications to set the story straight, to quickly respond, to pre-empt incidents, to make customers happy. In fact, if you were really smart, the Internet could potentially be a tool to generate advocacy, to take all those positive experiences and sentiments about your brand and share them with a larger audience.

The main lesson from the Kryptonite experience was simple but fundamental and resonates to this day. Make sure you are using the Internet to constantly monitor what people are saying about your brand, for better or worse. The Internet is full of chatter about topics, whether in social networks, communities, or specialized forums. Odds are someone is talking about your category, your competitors, your brand, your products, maybe even you.

Are You Responding?

Learning from the Kryptonite incident, many companies then took steps to ensure they would not be the next victims of a similar online failure. Remember all of those listening and monitoring programs I mentioned in chapter 2: Radian6, Brandwatch, Visible Technologies, and countless others? All of those tools and the real-time data that comes with them is just as if not more useful to other parts of the business outside the product development team. Your customer service and corporate communications teams in particular would find all of that customer chatter immensely helpful. So make sure you are freeing up the data, breaking down the silos, getting the right information to the right parts of your organization—and do it fast! If Kryptonite would have responded quickly to Chester Bullock rather than turning a blind eye, the company may have saved its reputation and a lot of stolen bikes. With the Internet you actually have the means to quickly respond either individually or at a larger scale to such issues or customer service needs. This communication is a two-way street, and as much as marketers want to use the Internet as the world's largest focus group, consumers want to use the Internet as the world's quickest way to solve problems.

For example, consider some recent American Express research on customer service. American Express tested over 1,500 consumers under various laboratory conditions to assess their reaction to various customer service conditions. Over 63 percent of those participants felt their heart rate increase when they thought about great customer service. In fact, 53 percent of them experienced the same brain reaction that you get when feeling loved. Alternatively, when consumers don't feel loved, things can go bad.[1] According to Accenture, 66 percent of global consumers switched brands or business due to poor customer service, a 4 percent increase over the figure of the previous year. Some 82 percent of the 66 percent who switched brands said the brand could have done something to stop them.[2] As an adaptive marketer, what steps are you taking to use real-time data to stop those dissatisfied customers about to switch to a competitor? Are you using the synchronous and instant data flow available on the Internet to quickly show your customers some love? Are you even aware that there are issues?

Unfortunately, for many companies the answer is still no, no, and no—at least according to consumers. While many companies might think they are excelling in customer service, most consumers still give them a failing grade. For example, the consulting firm Bain & Company reports that 80 percent of companies believe they offer "superior" customer service, but in reality only 8 percent of customers agree that this is the case.[3] Ironically, in many cases it's the very thing that should be helping you that is actually causing more problems. For when it comes to digital channels, many companies are still failing to keep up with that synchronous data exchange that more and more consumers are demanding. Back to Bain's researchers, who report that only 36 percent of consumers get an issue resolved quickly and effectively when they make some sort of customer service enquiry via sites like Facebook or Twitter. Worrying new research from Maritz found that of 1,298 Twitter complaints only 29 percent were replied to by the companies in question. In effect, over 70 percent of companies are simply ignoring customer complaints on Twitter.[4]

So many missed opportunities to show customers some love! Just a simple quick response would have done the trick. According to Maritz, 71 percent of those who received a quick and positive customer service response through social networks are likely to recommend that brand to others, compared to just 19 percent of customers who do not receive any response. The study found that 83 percent of the complainants who received a reply liked or loved the fact that the company responded, regardless of the timing or format of the response. It was simply the fact that someone at the company was listening, cared, and responded that made the biggest impact, which in the study improved customers' attitude 83 percent of the time. And these happy customers are willing to spend 20 percent to 40 per-cent more with that company.

Speed appears to be a recurring theme in all of these studies. In short, consumers expect a fast response when it comes to online customer service. According to data from the Social Habit, a social network research company, 42 percent of customers expect a company to respond to customer service issues within 60 minutes, and nearly 10 percent expect it within 5 minutes.[5] When it comes to Twitter, Millward Brown, a global research agency, claims that those expecting an answer within an hour increases to 72 percent.[6] Different people expect different response times on different social networks (see Figure 3.1). However, give or take a few minutes, they all expect a really fast response. As an adaptive marketer, your job is to make sure your company is adapting and responding as quickly as customers expect.

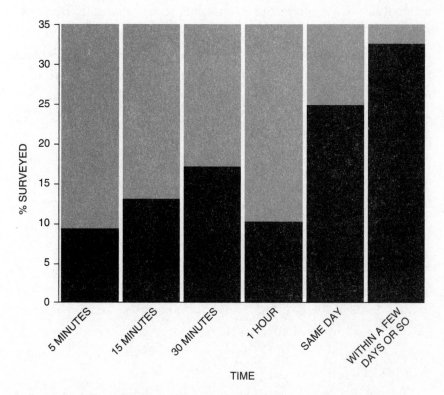

Figure 3.1 Response Time Expected by Companies Contacted on Social Media.
Source: Edison 2012.

Sometimes It Takes a Volcano

When the Icelandic volcano Eyjafjallajökull erupted in 2010, it also revolutionized the way KLM approached its customer service. With the volcano's ash plume spreading across Europe, Air Traffic Control, worried about engine safety, grounded and canceled flights across the continent, leaving thousands of helpless passengers stranded, struggling, and taking to social channels to commiserate and seek help. Viktor van der Wijk, director of digital marketing at Air France KLM, wisely put the company into the social slipstream to allow the brand to respond to customers in real time, helping and advising them on alternative travel options. Even when there was no solution to their problems, KLM customers knew the company was listening and doing everything it could to help them.

Since Eyjafjallajökull, KLM has made online and real-time social networks a core component of its customer service approach. Response rates to tweets and posts are now less than one hour, and all major issues are resolved within 24 hours. KLM is now on social analytics firm SocialBaker's leaderboard for its Facebook page response time to posts, with its most recent scores equating to an average response time of 99 minute and a 99 percent response rate to questions on the social platform (see Figure 3.2).

Nike is another example of a company using Twitter and synchronous data exchanges for customer service purposes. The Portland-based athletic apparel company set up @NikeSupport on Twitter as a destination for customers to get support on any Nike product, whether apparel or mobile applications. The answers to customer tweets are nearly instant and around the clock, seven days a week. Nike has even gone so far as to establish other Twitter handles and hashtags related to other parts of its business, but @NikeSupport has become the single, dedicated destination for customers to get an answer relating to any part of the business. By November,2014, @NikeSupport had more than 148,000 followers and nearly 350,000 tweets.

The mobile telecom giant O2 created a social media response team that uses live data streams from its RTO2 brand monitoring tool to

		FANS	RESPONSE TIME	RESPONSE RATE	ANSWERED MINUS IGNORED QUESTIONS
01	KLM	8 159 588	99 MIN	99.06 %	20 543
02	ROBI AXIATA LIMITED	2 471 429	20 MIN	98.97 %	19 573
03	GRAMEENPHONE	3 067 758	88 MIN	95.85 %	18 558
04	BANGLALINK MELA	2 400 611	41 MIN	98.84 %	11 670
05	TELKOMSEL	501 137	35 MIN	65.26 %	11 536
06	SAFARICOM KENYA OFFICIAL PAGE	1 000 376	10 MIN	98.74 %	8 203
07	ORANGE	1 713 515	16 MIN	99 %	6 590
08	YOUSEE	83 590	321 MIN	98.72 %	5 632
09	OPTUS	200 964	280 MIN	98.78 %	5 444
10	TELSTRA 24X7	547 522	77 MIN	98.01 %	5 350
	INDUSTRY BENCHMARK		1 721 MIN	68.56 %	

Figure 3.2 Top Ten Socially Devoted Brands.
Source: Socialbakers, 2014.

respond instantly to customer service needs. During a major two-day network outage in the United Kingdom, O2 used social channels extensively to respond to every customer inquiry and complaint as well as to provide up-to-the-minute updates on the situation. Over 30 team members worked day and night to keep the ten million customers of O2 updated and supported. O2 continues to use social channels as prime customer service destinations, and research has demonstrated that the customer satisfaction score for those interacting with O2 via networks like Twitter and Facebook is 73 compared to a score of 69 for those who do not.[7] In effect, real-time adaptive customer service increased overall customer satisfaction scores by 6 percent.

Another example is Next, a large multinational British retailer of clothing, footwear, and home products that also has a large online store; it has made its way up to the top adaptive customer service brands. Next's customer service team has used Facebook extensively to help customers directly rather than simply sending them to a website or customer service number. Within 36 minutes, over 87 percent of Facebook fan posts are resolved by a representative, often by direct or private messages within Facebook until the issue has been settled.

The companies listed on the SocialBaker's social response time leaderboard, including KLM, represent some of the finest examples of marketers boldly embracing online synchronous social channels to respond quickly to customer service needs. But how do you determine where you want to establish a customer service outpost given the growing number of social networks available to marketers and consumers? Facebook and Twitter tend to be the most obvious networks given their respective scale and sustained success. However, even within those two environments, there are nuances in how consumers use them. For example, Twitter tends to be a destination for people to respond to a live event or larger issue either individually or as a collective group, frequently around hashtags; as many companies have discovered, these are difficult to control. In contrast, Facebook is a more controlled environment, and for companies and their brands it is increasingly a paid media platform rather than a place for creating organic advocacy and word-of-mouth advertising for the brand.

In the end, every company needs to go through the due diligence on understanding these different social networks, particularly as new players emerge, existing ones evolve, and consumer behavior changes. Here are some tips when considering your options.

Tops Tips for Establishing a Customer Service Outpost

1. Identify where your customers spend time. Which social networks do they currently use? Do significant numbers spend significant time on the network? Does it give you large enough scale across multiple markets?
2. Determine whether that's where customers want to engage with you. Just because they spend time somewhere doesn't necessarily mean they want to spend time there with you. While teens may

use SnapChat extensively, they are most likely not using it for customer service issues.

3. Ensure the social network has longevity. Has the network proven that it will stand the test of time, or is it merely this year's passing fad? Is it worth the investment in time and capital?

4. In any case, above all protect the brand. Ensure that you own your brand's footprint in all social networks regardless as to whether you want to activate it or not. You don't want an imposter seemingly speaking on behalf of your brand.

5. Understand the nuances. Whether it's expected response time or communication best practice, opportunities, and limits (just 140 characters per tweet!) ensure you are adapting your approach to each social network's unique behavioral traits.

Tapping into Your Inner Geek

Like many college students, Robert Stephens desperately needed to bring in some money to help fund his college education. Rather than work at a local restaurant or video rental shop, Stephens decided to tap into his inner geek and help people fix their technology. Using his bike, Stephens would make house or office calls to those struggling to set up a newly purchased TV or fix a faulty computer. To Stephens's delight he discovered there were lots of people completely bewildered by all this newfangled technology, people willing to pay decent money to have a geek visit them to solve their problems. Complex technology + hapless consumers + geek = money.

Giant consumer electronics retailer Best Buy noticed the same problem. Even with the clearest of instructions, consumers still found it a real nightmare to install or activate what they had just purchased at the store. The inevitable outcome was a deluge of desperate pleas from befuddled Best Buy customers.

To answers this collective cry for help, the managers at Best Buy decided to tap into their inner geek. In short, Best Buy decided to buy Stephens' company for $3 million, instantly creating an army of geeks willing to help their technically disinclined neighbors. Soon "Chief

Inspector" Robert Stephens and his Geek Squad were providing Best Buy customers with support in the store, on the website, over the phone, even at their location. The Geek Squad, in the words of Best Buy, were people who could "swap a motherboard or hook up a home theatre system blindfolded."[8] Best Buy scaled the organization by screening and signing up nerds from the around the country. They selected those who passed the geek test to join this service group, available to Best Buy consumers at various membership schemes to help them online with any technology issues they may be facing.

The Geek Squad is now over 24, 000 individuals strong, and according to private equity speculation, it makes billions in annual revenue. Geek Squad cars can be seen all over the United States zipping around towns to help anguished civilians looking for technical assistance. The program is a great example of using real-time data, in this case synchronous consumer dialogues with Best Buy, to instantly connect people with other people, in this case the right expert to help them immediately solve issues. It's adaptive customer service in real-time action.

All of this effort hopefully helps retain customers and also turns them into advocates; both are important achievements. According to eConsultancy, 70 percent of UK companies say it's cheaper to retain a customer than acquire a new one.[9] Furthermore, if those customers become advocates, we know that their support on networks like Facebook and Twitter via sharing and retweeting has a significant impact on their friends, on average more so than paid advertising. According to Syncapse, a social media marketing management company, fans of a product are 41 percent more likely than other people to recommend it to friends. Once these folks become fans, they spend on average an additional $71.84 than those who are not fans.[10] Furthermore, research done by TNS shows that word-of-mouth advertising is twice as powerful as advertising in getting customers to try a product.[11]

The power of word-of-mouth advertising is just one reason why so many companies, such as Best Buy, are building their online customer service right into social networks like Facebook and Twitter. By doing so, they provide customers with an easy and quick way to connect with a brand, share a customer service need, and in most cases get a quick response from the company or from other consumers who just happen to have passed the geek test. As an added bonus, most of these social networks are designed for mobile devices, making it easy for customers to engage while on the move.

One of the key components of successful online customer service in social networks like Facebook and Twitter is to have the underlying technology that enables you to manage the data and conversations and to have the ability to publish content quickly across the various social outposts you've created, including targeting the content by language and market. As with social listening tools, you need to think carefully about selecting your technology, particularly as, according to Salesforce.com, the most successful and cost-effective implementations tend to be at the enterprise level, that is, across business divisions and markets. Some of the more popular industry tools at the time of publishing include Salesforce's own Marketing Cloud as well as Hootsuite, Sprinklr, Sprout Social, and Tweetdeck.

Common Criteria for Social Management and Publishing Tools

1. With which social networks does the tool operate? Can it publish on multiple social networks, or does it only work with the big networks like Facebook and Twitter?
2. Does it work across languages and markets? Does the tool have the ability to manage (publish, republish) content across multiple markets? Does it work in different languages?
3. What incremental features does the tool include? How sophisticated are the analytics and reporting? Does it integrate with your existing CRM systems and web publishing platforms?
4. How open is the technology? If it's missing critical features, can you integrate the technology with other tools in your adaptive technology stack, such as your analytics and social listening tools?
5. How advanced and secure are the administrative controls? Does the tool have the necessary controls to ensure content can be approved? How secure is the system from hackers?

One Person Can Make a Difference

Most of the examples we've seen so far illustrate companies using social networks and synchronous data exchanges to help solve customers' needs. However, as in the Kryptonite example, sometimes companies are simply confronted with a good old-fashioned crisis. Such was the case for British Petroleum (BP) during the 2010 Gulf of Mexico oil spill off the coast of Texas. The Deepwater Horizon accident was the biggest offshore oil disaster in the history of the United States, and with 11 deaths and extensive environmental damage, it stirred up a tidal wave of discussion online, most of it highly negative to BP. Whether the accident was BP's fault or a supplier's was irrelevant; local citizens were angry and expected answers from someone. This ensuing online discussion flooded social networks and TV news channels and quickly led to a 2 percent drop in BP's stock price.

To BP's credit, the company did respond. In addition to mobilizing a cleanup effort in the Gulf, BP also mobilized an adaptive customer service and corporate communications team completely focused on ensuring there was nonstop communication of its efforts and the facts associated with the spill. The latter was extraordinarily important given the amount of conjecture and false information being spread on social media. BP took people from various parts of its business and established a real-time communications team in a mission control centre in Texas, where the group quickly started to respond and adapt BP's communications to reflect the news and conversation happening in real time both online and offline.

BP purchased the words most frequently entered into Google on topics related to the oil spill and made sure people could find a link providing details and facts on the cleanup efforts and the accident's underlying causes. BP set up Twitter and Facebook outposts to respond to consumers in real time, frequently scrambling to find information based on trending topics and issues. BP even monitored TV news channels and coverage, instantly tweeting data and information in response to television debates, particularly when inaccurate information was being provided.

Despite all the steps taken, BP still struggled when it came to winning the public relations war over the oil spill. Arguably, this was a battle the company was never going to win. Perhaps it was always going to be a question of minimizing the damage. Part of the issue was cutting through the confusion and noise being generated online, some of this was coming from a fake BP Twitter account called @BPGlobalPR, which ended up having five times as many followers as the official BP Twitter account. Lesson #1: Make sure you own all of your brand-related social handles.

Perhaps the biggest issue and learning was how a difference in approach across the organization could lead to mixed messages, particularly between the online social efforts and the broader PR disaster forming around BP's CEO, who showed little remorse or empathy regarding the situation. CEO Tony Hayward seemed more interested in sailing than in spending time supporting efforts to clean up the mess. Hayward ultimately lost his job, but he single-handedly created immense PR difficulties for BP. Lesson #2: With all the efforts and investment in the world, one bad move, or many in this case, by a CEO or even a rogue junior employee can cause immense damage.

For example, Barilla's CEO Guido Barilla made an off-the-cuff but very public remark to a journalist on the Italian Radio24 show *La Zanzara*. Barilla said that his company would not be featuring gay people in its ads because he supports traditional families. In his words, "if they disagree, they can go eat another brand of pasta."[12] Of course, his comments were deeply insulting to the LGBT community as well as to the many other consumers who support that group's rights to equality. Within a short time a protest community was formed online called #boycottabarilla, which quickly became a trending topic on Twitter and gained widespread publicity, all of it deeply embarrassing for the Barilla company and its brand.

To Guido Barilla's credit, he soon apologized on Twitter for his remarks, issuing a statement of regret for his offence that clearly stated that he respected everyone. However, by the time he humbly apologized, #boycottabarilla had led to an online petition to boycott the brand, which ended up getting over 123,000 signatures.

Barilla's mishap was a real-time adaptive opportunity for the pasta maker's competition. Buitoni, a competing pasta brand owned by Nestlé, quickly responded to the situation by posting a simple image on Facebook stating "PastaForAll" and featuring some same sex pasta gender symbols. In short, Buitoni raised its brand's voice in support of the LGBT community, earning widespread positive word-of-mouth advertising and advocacy on Twitter and elsewhere. One brand's misfortune ended up being another company's opportunity to reinforce its brand image and generate some positive vibes.[13]

Ultimately, the total impact of this incident on sales for either Barilla or Buitoni is less clear. According to Spire, a global research and consulting firm, both Barilla sales and buyers remained fairly consistent year-on-year following the incident. BP, on the other hand, saw its share price more than halve before the end of its disastrous 2010. Lesson #3: Unlike BP's Tony Hayward, Guido Barilla with his quick attempt to rectify the situation perhaps saved the company from a lingering PR disaster. Sometimes one person can really make a difference, in good ways *and* bad.

Accidents Will Happen

Nestlé is one company that has been extremely ambitious in building an ongoing dialogue with its customers that covers everything from promotional contests to tackling service problems. For the most part, Nestlé has earned rave reviews for its handling of some difficult issues raised on public sites such as Facebook and Twitter, which had not always been the case. For example, way back in 2010 a controversy erupted online over Nestlé's use of palm oil in its Kit Kat confectionary products. Within a few weeks, a group of environmentalists had made a concentrated effort to publically criticize Nestlé's supposed sourcing of palm oil from an Indonesian company that was known for causing widespread ecological damage to rainforests, home of endangered orangutans. The protesters posted highly damaging YouTube videos, bombarded the Kit Kat Facebook pages, and brewed up a storm on Twitter.

Since that incident and soon after joining the company, Pete Blackshaw, Nestlé's global vice president of digital and social media, introduced robust guidelines, technology, and training to ensure Nestlé's brand teams, markets, and its wider agency ecosystem were prepared to handle such situations. Blackshaw's efforts led to him being inducted into the Word of Mouth Marketing Association's Hall of Fame in 2014. In short, Blackshaw and Nestlé know what they are doing when it comes to social marketing.

However, even with all the protocols and safety measures in the world, accidents can still happen. In 2014 a major controversy erupted in the United States over the National Football Association's apparent indifference to several players' abuse of their spouses and partners. When a video emerged of NFL player Ray Rice punching his fiancé, thousands of women went to Twitter to share their personal experiences of domestic abuse. While Ray Price was suspended, the controversy around the NFL and the wider discussion of the issue grew significantly around a hashtag called #WhyIStayed, where women shared gut-wrenching experiences and attempted to support each other.

Meanwhile, the social community manager at Nestlé's pizza brand DiGiorno posted a light-hearted tweet inadvertently using the #WhyIStayed hashtag (#WhyIStayed You Had Pizza). Within minutes, the DiGiorno tweet stirred up a massive wave of retweeted disgust and disappointment. How could a pizza brand social manager find any humor in such a serious social issue? The DiGiorno marketing team quickly realized the mistake and deleted the tweet and subsequently issued an apology: "A million apologies. Did not read what the hashtag was about before posting."[14]

All of Blackshaw's success in turning Nestlé into one of the Internet's premier social marketers was abruptly stopped by this single tweet. All the training and protocols hadn't anticipated such a blunder. Or maybe they had? Maybe Blackshaw and Nestlé knew that sometimes mistakes happen, and it is how the brand responds in these circumstances that really counts.

Other companies, including snack manufacturer brand Entenmann's, have made similar mistakes, and have either shut down their social media footprint or attempted to ride out the controversy with silence. To Nestlé and DiGiorno's credit, the company did the opposite in this situation. The DiGiorno community manager who made the mistake in the first place and who was clearly devastated, reached out personally to every individual who had tweeted in disgust and personally apologized to these people. Tweet after tweet, the community manager simply said "sorry, it was an unintended accident."

People listened. What had started as a potentially major PR disaster and embarrassment for the brand ended up within 24 hours turning into a wave of empathy and encouragement as the tide of opinion on Twitter turned, and people realized a genuine mistake had been made by a real person. In the words of Kimberly-Clark's Chris Whalen, when a brand such as Nestlé's DiGiorno responds in an "authentic" way, people respond positively.

Despite the best guardrails in the world, accidents will happen. In 2014, the US Airways community manager accidently tweeted a link to a pornographic image in response to a customer who was complaining about a flight delay. US Airways quickly apologized and deleted the post. The anniversary of the September 11 terrorist attack has become another accident-prone territory for companies to do dumb things. Retailer Build-a-Bear tweeted an image of one of its teddy bears wearing a camouflage outfit and some dog tags. The motto "We will never forget" accompanied the image. The Build-a-Bear folks quickly realized that the post was in poor taste. In general, it is tricky for companies to try and insert their brands into national tragedies.

Accidents happen, but that doesn't mean you should pack up your bags and give up on Facebook and Twitter. Whether you like it or not, consumers generally expect brands to have an online and social media presence and be responsive. Rather than considering social networks opportunities to fail, marketers should see them as golden opportunities to succeed fast by implicitly listening to online chatter via brand monitoring or by directly engaging with consumers in a dialogue. In both situations, arguably more so in explicit communications, the brand's personality and voice and the rules that govern when and how it engages with consumers will be more important than ever. And just as brands can capitalize on real-time events, marketers must also be prepared for any accidents that may occur and may require adapting in a very different way.

Finding Your Brand's Voice

Like many fathers, when the New York Mets second baseman Daniel Murphy had his newborn baby son Noah, he decided to take a few days off on paternity leave. Unfortunately for Daniel, his paternity leave was right in the middle of the baseball season, and this caused an uproar among some fans and pundits. Soon Twitter was full of abusive trolls, tweeting statements such as: "Why should he need to be there for more than one day. It's not like he is breastfeeding. What is he doing?"[15]

The marketers of Kimberly-Clark's Huggies brand saw this as an opportunity to validate the brand's positioning, in particular its support for both new moms *and* new dads. In this case it wasn't a competitor's stumble but a trending news story that provided the company with an opportunity to send a message that not only is it alright for dads to take some time off when they have a new baby, but that such parental leave should be encouraged. Huggies posted messages of solidarity and support to Daniel Murphy and other new dads on its Facebook and Twitter accounts and offered to donate diapers to the National Diaper Bank Network for each use and share of the hashtag #HuggiesSupportsDaniel. This simple post, which took the Huggies team a few hours to create, ended up receiving nearly 90,000 likes, retweets, shares, and favorites on Facebook and Twitter. The result was that many underprivileged newborn babies and toddlers received much-needed diapers, and all due to a simple post and the goodwill of many Facebook and Twitter users.

According to Chris Whalen, while overall this tweet was a big success for Huggies, the marketing team still learnt many lessons from this early foray into real time. "Our adaptive muscles weren't quite there yet, we were still in a learning mode to work out when and how the brand should respond to these types of situations," says Whalen when reflecting on the Daniel Murphy post. Simple things such as using the image of an African-American man for the father rather than Murphy's actual image (Kimberly-Clark didn't own the rights) stirred up some minor backlash. "This is what Daniel Murphy looks like," one Facebook user posted with an image of the baseball player. Whalen is sanguine about such situations and considers them positive learning that accumulates and gets codified and subsequently shared across the company.

The learnings from the Daniel Murphy situation later came in handy for Huggies in Hong Kong when information reached the marketing team that a diaper bank had been robbed resulting in the loss of thousands of diapers. The Huggies team used social networks to swiftly work with the local community to replace every diaper lost. Huggies volunteered to match each of the reward points donated by consumers so that "every little bottom" in Hong Kong would have a diaper. There was no paid promotion behind the response, which became a trending story not only online but also in the mainstream press, including on the television news. Huggies, which is a challenger brand in Hong Kong, ended up dominating its competitors and gaining significant kudos from the community for coming to the rescue quicker than anyone else.

Whalen cites many key learnings from both the Hong Kong and the Daniel Murphy events. According to Whalen, "the fact that Huggies was being true to its brand voice by being authentic versus self-serving was of primary importance." Whalen says speed and response time were also key factors. "In Hong Kong our competitors also eventually helped replenish the diaper bank, but the fact that we were first meant Huggies got the bulk of the publicity and public recognition for taking those first steps to help."

Whalen believes that to succeed in adaptive and dynamic environments like Facebook and Twitter, marketers need to carefully define their brand's personality and voice as well as the appropriate occasions and rules for when and how to speak to and engage with a wider audience. Some of these moments may be positive or negative, corporate or cultural. Such external events and data can be used to prepare a brand for potential customer service issues or even to inject the brand into a situation where it can play a relevant role in proactively help-ing and supporting people from the broader perspective of corporate responsibility.

It is important to keep in mind that without such clear guidelines and accumulated learning, marketing teams can do some pretty dumb things. For example, consider the 2012 World Cup competition. Various national airlines used the results of the football tournament to communicate with their customers. For example, KLM celebrated the Dutch team's victory over Mexico with a quick tweet stating "Adios Amigos"; the tweet featured some stereotypical imagery of sombre-ros, serape blankets, and mustaches. The tweet was highly offensive to Mexicans, who promptly took it viral under the hashtag #mexi-cogate. Mexican actor Gael Garcia Bernal didn't mince words with KLM, tweeting what most of his compatriots felt: "I'm never flying your shitty airline again. F—— you big time." Bernal happens to have two million Twitter followers.

In contrast, Brussels Airlines humbly celebrated Belgium's defeat of the US team by giving all travelers on its flights to and from the United States a box of Belgian chocolates with a small card stating "Thanks for the match of a lifetime. We hope we can become your favourite country again soon." The accompanying #BELUSA hashtag sparked a frenzy of customer love, particularly from gracious Americans still recovering from a tough loss against the Belgian Red Devils football team.

Lesson #4: stay true to your brand's personality, particularly when events occur where you wish to give your brand a voice. When done poorly or out of character, such misguided brand responses can back-fire. However, when done appropriately, customers overall seem to wel-come your brand's voice and the communication. A Harris Interactive survey of more than 2,000 consumers found that 87 percent of adults in the United States are open to being proactively contacted by a brand when it comes to service and support.[16] Nearly three-quarters of those who have had a pleasant surprise or positive experience with proactive communication from a company report they also had a positive change in their perception of that organization and its brand.

In short, the vast majority of customers have a positive view of proactive customer service and support from a company and its brands based on adaptive situations. Unfortunately, according to Forrester Research's Forrsights Networks and Telecommunications Survey, only 29 percent of companies are investing in such proactive and adaptive outbound communications.[17]

Real Love in Real Places

Most of us have seen the long lines snaking out of retail stores when a new phone or gadget or gaming console goes on sale. Many of us have stood in those lines, which can start forming days in advance of the product being released for sale. This was the situation when the new Microsoft Xbox One went on sale in 2014. Long lines of Xbox gaming fanatics formed, all of them waiting for the long anticipated console to finally become available.

Of course, when you are standing in such a long line you have lots of downtime. Equipped with mobile phones, most of these Xboxers ended up going online to tweet about their excitement to their fellow gamers and the wider Xbox community. But it wasn't just enthusiasm they shared, it was also hunger. Standing in line, sometimes overnight, inevitably leads to dwindling food supplies and a growing appetite. Eventually, a few of these gamers sent a desperate tweet pleading for some food.

The Xbox Elite Tweet Fleet picked up on these rumbling tummies as they monitored the Twitter feeds coming in from around the world. The Elite Tweet Fleet isn't just any old team; these guys are some of the best, if not the very best, when it comes to real-time response. This team posts an average of about 4,000 tweets a day, most of them responding to roughly 5,000 customer support questions from gamers. The average response time is two minutes and 42 seconds, which makes the team, according to the *Guinness World Records*, the most "Most Responsive Brand on Twitter."[18]

So how did this elite team respond to those hungry consumers requesting some food while waiting in line for their new Xbox One console? By sending some pizza, of course. The team arranged for some pizzas to be delivered to these fanatical Xboxers standing in line on a cold November evening in London. Lesson #5: sometimes online data and information can be used to proactively create a little bit of physical delight for customers.

Microsoft Xbox is not the only company using online data to proactively please customers and improve customer service. Britain's BT (British Telecommunications) has developed a tool called "Debatescape" that does a similar job as Radian6 in listening to what customers and noncustomers are saying about the brand and its products and services. However, BT does more than just listening. It is using its Debatescape tool to proactively find people who are having issues, even those who haven't yet contacted BT, and then reaching out to them to help solve those problems. The net effect has been an improvement in savings, higher customer satisfaction, and reduced customer churn. In short, BT uses real-time data to proactively identify those customers who need some love and then quickly reaches out to them.

Some companies are using this listening data to adapt their customer service content, whether online or in their customer service call centers. Janssen Pharmaceuticals takes the data it picks up from brand monitoring and uses it to inform the content development required for its online customer service, whether including new FAQs or eliminating jargon that turned out to create confusion. The company also equips its medical information call centers with all of this information, knowing that there is an increased likelihood that related customer needs and questions may start coming in over the phone lines. Overall, the Janssen team has analyzed over 54,000 online conversations, and the corresponding content changes ended up improving revisit rates to the company's website by 20 percent, taking pressure and costs off its call centers.[19]

The Dutch airline KLM, perhaps in attempt to make up for its misguided tweet about the Mexican World Cup team, launched its highly ambitious #happytohelp online customer service initiative in 2014. Over 250 customer service representatives are now busy working around the clock in an effort to answer each and every customer inquiry the company receives.

Similar to Xbox, BT, and Janssen, the team uses real-time online data to rapidly adapt the customer experience both online and in the real world. Sitting in their mission control center, the #happytohelp staff are creating all types of content, including YouTube videos, in response to a variety of customer needs, including tourist tips for cities, visa requirements, and flight changes.

Arguably, it's the real-world experiences where KLM is really going out of its way. KLM has helped travelers stuck in bad traffic on the way to the airport by hiring motorbikes and speed boats to transport them quickly. KLM has been known to fetch forgotten passports from homes on behalf of its panicked customers at the airport. The #happytohelp staff even made a wake-up tweet and call over the phone and offered breakfast at the airport to a traveler who had to get up early to catch her flight. Perhaps to make up for their tweet about the Mexican World Cup team, KLM also recorded a video with personalized Spanish language lessons for a traveler flying to Mexico. How the Mexican actor Gael Garcia Bernal, formerly so irate at KLM, responded is unclear, but overall the program was a big hit for the airline and, more important, for its customers.

Smart adaptive marketers are using online marketing not only to respond to customer service issues through networks like Twitter and Facebook, but also to integrate that data into all parts of the customer service organization, including call centers. Some companies are even going so far as to proactively preempt problems and delight customers, everything from feeding hungry customers with pizzas to getting them to the airport via a speedboat. Despite the problems and accidents that will inevitably occur, online and its synchronous real-time data provides a powerful if not increasingly necessary means to keep your customers happy and to avoid all the lessons and spectacular failures experienced by so many other unwitting companies and marketers over the years (see Figure 3.3). Yes, you may fail fast in some cases, but you can also succeed fast as well.

	LISTEN	ENGAGE	CUSTOMIZE
APPROACH	Use social data and outposts to identify, listen to and solve customer services issues.	Inject the brand's voice into a positive or negative event directly or indirectly related to the brand.	Use data to generate customer love through customized content and experiences both online and offline
LEADERS	Nike, O2, KLM	Kimberly-Clark, BP, Buitoni	Xbox, KLM, Janssen, BT
PRO'S	Consumers increasingly expect brands to listen to them in social networks and then help them solve problems.	Opportunity to mitigate issues or build broader advocacy by helping customers and/or demonstrating the brand's values.	Who doesn't love a pizza or speed boat? Shows customers you are proactively solving their needs either online, on the phone or in real life.
CON'S	Normally requires time, energy, and investment to be successful. Plus it's not just about listening. People want you to respond with solutions...quickly.	Requires clarity and discipline around the brand's voice and real-time response parameters, including decision-making. Even with all of that accidents can still happen.	Can be costly. Ensure you factor in the scope of what you are promising.

Figure 3.3 Different Adaptive Approaches for Customer Service.

In the next chapter we will take a look at how adaptive marketers are using the different qualities and quantities of data to adapt their advertising, both the creative part and the media.

Top Tips for Using Data to Delight Consumers

1. Clarify your online customer service outposts. Make sure customers know where, how, and when you will respond to customer

service issues. Set expectations on response times and meet them. If your Facebook brand page is not the right place, let customers know where to go.

2. Expect the unexpected. On the other hand, you can't stop people from tweeting and posting about your company and potential customer service issues. Even if you are not formally responding on sites like Facebook, you need to be prepared to respond and react to customers following their own rules, including when they want to break them—and you.

3. Respond fast. Don't stick your head in the sand. Don't bury bad news. Get back to your customers quickly, either individually or a wider audience if it's an issue affecting lots of people. If you don't, the problem will only get worse.

4. Share the love. Encourage your customers to share their love for your brand with others. Happy customers not only spend more money, they also spread positive word-of-mouth comments to other potential new customers.

5. Be true to your brand voice. Make sure you understand the brand's personality and how it would respond to customers in real-time, real-life situations. In most cases it's not a good idea to come across as inauthentic and impersonal.

CHAPTER 3.1

The Change Agent on Data
Nathan Summers, Global Head of Digital and CRM
Jaguar Land Rover

When I started in my new role at Jaguar Land Rover (JLR), I knew I didn't have much time to ease into the position. Things were changing fast in the automotive industry, and it was imperative that the company rapidly put in a new enterprise infrastructure that would lay the foundation for JLR's future ambitions. Just like it builds high-performance engines for its cars, JLR had to build a high-performance adaptive engine for its marketing.

Just consider dealership visits, which according to McKinsey had significantly declined from an average of 5 to 1.4 visits, which means consumers were doing more of their research online and less of it on the ground. And this research wasn't even happening on the old Internet, but instead on mobile devices. According to Google, 62 percent of the target consumers are now using their phone as the start point of search activity. Emboldened by this research and data, the JLR leadership team knew that we had to change the way we understand and interact with empowered current and potential customers, who now make most of their key decisions in the digital space.

To succeed in the future, digital could no longer be just advertising and websites; digital and it's rich data and synchronous data flow had to become a much more effective way of managing the whole experience throughout the car buying journey leading all the way to a sale and even beyond into service and support. Underpinning the firm's digital agenda is indeed that smart data set, which sits at the center of JLR's enterprise infrastructure. This data enables JLR to develop a deep understanding of individual customer journeys, the successive content needed to fit these journeys, and the dynamic technology platforms required to enable content to behave adaptively.

By 2014, we had launched the company's boldest effort in digital to date, a new dynamic consumer-facing web infrastructure for LandRover.com and Jaguar.com. Both platforms were designed with smart screens at the heart of the interaction, providing the ability to integrate paid, owned, and earned content to drive efficiency in customers' experience and communications. But there was more to the websites than just an innovative brand experience. The team had also implemented a robust enterprise analytics suite, further enhanced by anonymous event tracking and behavioral targeting across millions of interactions (online impressions). As a result JLR, through additional third-party data sets, is now able to get a much richer understanding of those who engage with the brand, including their age, gender, education, and household income. The cumulative outcome is an incredibly rich outline of the company's consumers, both at an aggregated and at an individual level. All of this data can then be made available via detailed analytics reports, real-time dashboards, and geospatial modeling tools, helping JLR gain truly multidimensional insights obtained at both macro and micro levels.

A myriad of use cases continue to emerge from this data, which has helped JLR adapt many elements of its marketing activities, everything from global advertising campaigns to dealership promotions. For example, the data helped JLR understand which online brand videos performed best at the time of nameplate reveal and what other vehicles in the Jaguar portfolio also drew a reaction from the audience. The adaptive and practical applications of this were the optimization of those assets, the ability to feed factual insights into the advertising briefing (e.g., aluminum is a strong story that should be reprised in advertising), and finally the evidence to prove that communication about one nameplate can actually act as a "hero" or bridge to take consumers to other nameplates that perhaps better suit their budget or lifestyle.

Our ability to implement an integrated and robust adaptive technology across JLR continues to show promise as more data is parsed, scrutinized, and acted upon across the organization. At a minimum, this technology has given the JLR marketing community not only the means but also an incentive to measure all of the communications throughout the JLR business. We continue to enrich the data set, most recently integrating this new unified consumer intelligence across all channels with JLR's SAP CRM platform and its new programmatic advertising platform.

It's been a challenging journey at times, but it is one well worth the effort since we are now in a better position to get closer to the customer than ever before and move faster than our competition.

CHAPTER 4

Exploring the Spectrum

You have now seen how smart adaptive marketers are tapping into the power of real-time data to quickly gain insight into customers' needs and then use that information to inform and improve products and customer service. You've also seen the wide spectrum of adaptive opportunities available to marketers, everything from Netflix's subtle use of viewing data to develop new original programming to #KLM #happytohelp's not so subtle use of a speedboat to help a tweeting customer stuck in a traffic jam. Adaptive marketing is a pretty big sandbox to play in, full of opportunities to apply data in new and creative ways, and nothing illustrates that more than the world of advertising.

Traffic, Temperature, and Trains

Most have us have seen our fair share of traffic jams in life. For many people living in urban areas sitting in traffic has become a rush hour ritual. You sit in your car and slowly progress along the highway while listening to the morning DJ or perhaps sneaking a peek at your mobile phone for incoming e-mails. Rush hour has become forced downtime in an increasingly hectic world of multi-everything.

Still, even traffic jams can be an opportunity, for when you are stuck on the highway, you actually have some time to take a look at your surroundings, perhaps to absorb a little more than you would if you were speeding by at 55 miles an hour. The credit goes to networking equipment giant

Cisco for cleverly picking up on this enforced downtime and deciding to capitalize on it to promote its "Tomorrow Starts Here" initiative, a campaign promoting the products and services of the Internet of Things.

Cisco erected an outdoor billboard along one of Silicon Valley's busier roads and then adapted the creative ad presented there based on the traffic speed on the highway. If traffic was moving very fast the billboard reduced the content to one key simple message that most drivers could read even at over 55 miles an hour ("The Internet of Everything is changing everything"). As average speeds decreased, more content was placed on the billboard, because Cisco knew that drivers going at say 30 miles per hour could take in more information ("The Internet of Everything is changing this billboard based on your speed"). Finally, at speeds less than 20 miles per hour, Cisco delivered the full amount of text ("The Internet of Everything is changing this billboard based on your speed. So you only see what you have time to read," which was followed by a short statement: "Sorry about the slow going."). It was a simple but highly adaptive way to promote Cisco's hyperconnected Internet of Things message, and it was all based on once piece of real-time data: your traffic speed.

Cisco is not the first company to come up with an adaptive outdoor campaign. In fact, many companies have used that time-tested data feed, the weather, to adapt the creative messaging appearing before drivers. For example, JCDecaux's outdoor digital team used a local weather data feed to change the content of Leinenkugel's Summer Shandy beer billboards in Chicago. Regardless of whether the weather was rainy, sunny, or cloudy, there was always some variant of shandy that could be promoted based on the conditions outside. One small piece of data, one very clever variation in the creative message.

Stella Artois experimented with a similar outdoor campaign for its Cidre alcohol brand, which is normally consumed on hot summer days. Rather than changing the content as Leinenkugel did, Stella Artois used the temperature to determine whether to even run the outdoor advertisement. Once again, using a real-time weather data feed, Posterscope, a network of outdoor sites, used a real-time temperature feed to activate the Cidre ads only when the temperature rose two degrees or more above the average in any specific location. If the temperature remained below a predetermined average, then the ads did not appear. This means that people in Cidre's target audience saw the ads only when they were hot and presumably thirsty. One small piece of data, one very clever variation in the media plan.

Swedish hair-care company Apotek Hjärtat tapped into another source of real-time data to develop an adaptive subway poster ad for its Apolosophy product range. Apotek built in sensor technology into the posters to detect when subway trains entered the station, which then triggered the hair on the ad's female models to blow around much like it would do in real life.

In all of these cases there was no big data involved. Instead, these smart marketers used one key but important data source to adapt either the creative message or the media placement to make the advertising more impactful and relevant to the target audience.

The Spectrum

Outdoor is one of many areas of advertising that is in the process of being reinvented and revolutionized by data and digital. In fact, most analog channels such as TV, print, radio are all evolving as they become plugged into the Internet or adopt new digital technologies. Even with all this change, for the most part there remains a stubborn border between the highly adaptive world of online advertising and the relatively inflexible world of off-line media, although the two are increasingly connected in various ways.

Rob Norman, Chief Digital Officer (CDO) of WPP Group's GroupM, believes these two divergent types of media can be called the "adaptive layer" and the "foundational layer." According to Norman, "the adaptive layer consists of media that can be quickly changed based on fast incoming data and evolving circumstances... think of Twitter, Facebook, Google search... while the foundational layer consists of the analogue media that have historically dominated, for example, the big creative TV spot that may be the cornerstone of any new product launch."[1] In contrast to the off-line foundational layer, the new

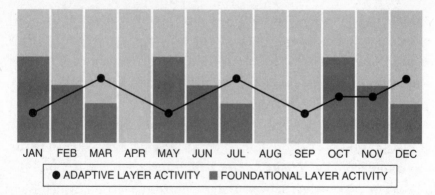

JAN FEB MAR APR MAY JUN JUL AUG SEP OCT NOV DEC

● ADAPTIVE LAYER ACTIVITY   ■ FOUNDATIONAL LAYER ACTIVITY

Figure 4.1   The Foundational and Adaptive Layers of Media.

adaptive layer is not only mostly digital, it is also typically "always on," sustaining ongoing brand communications in between the foundational bursts that take place throughout the year (see Figure 4.1).

What's important to note is that these two layers are increasingly blurring into one single adaptive layer, largely depending on your location in the world. As we saw in chapter 1, cheap, ubiquitous, and fast Internet access usually translates into rapid change while the opposite equates to a more glacial pace of evolution. Regardless, the direction of the trends across markets is similar; everything, everywhere is becoming more adaptive, just at different speeds.

So what are the current key trends within and between these two layers?

First, most marketers are moving more of their media spend into the "adaptive layer" primarily due to the fact that consumers are spending more time on the Internet, either on their computers or, increasingly, on mobile devices. Consequently, for marketers to reach their targeted audiences, they need to essentially "fish where the fish are," which happens to be the Internet. This is particularly true of digital natives, the younger generation whose members are spending a disproportionate amount of time online, often on social sites such as Snapchat, Twitch, and Steam. However, the shift to the adaptive layer is also happening because marketers are attracted to digital media's ability to make changes faster, whether by changing media investment or the creative messages. All this makes marketing resonate more with consumers and ultimately drives up return on investment (ROI).

A second trend is that the foundational layer is increasingly connected to the adaptive layer. The two don't exist in isolation. Indeed, they are more interconnected than ever before. According to the global information and measurement company Nielsen, 86 percent of mobile Internet users in the United States now watch TV with their mobile devices in hand; a trend that is being repeated elsewhere in the world.[2] A study by Kantar, a global research and data consulancy, consisting of over 55,000 Internet users worldwide discovered that almost half the people (48 percent) who watch TV in the evening simultaneously engage in other online activities, including socializing, sending messages, and shopping.[3] So while this multiscreening growth is nuanced and different depending on the market, primarily based on smartphone or feature phone penetration levels, in general the trend toward a highly connected and adaptive media experience is on the rise.

A third and final trend is that the foundational layer itself is going through an evolution to become part of a singular adaptive layer as all media becomes digital. Many years ago Gartner, an IT research and consultancy company, came up with its "IP-enabled Gene Theory," which accurately stated that once a device becomes connected to the Internet, consumer usage permanently evolves albeit in nuanced and different ways compared to that of other digital devices. Mobile phones are one spectacular example; once Internet access was available on your phone, it forever changed your experience with the device but perhaps not in the same way as you used the Internet on the computer.

Arguably, we may be witnessing the death throes of the foundational layer as more devices get plugged into the Internet and start adopting digital and adaptive characteristics. Look at TV, arguably the big kahuna of the foundational layer (see Figure 4.2). According to BGR, a mobile and technology news source, over 87 million Smart Internet-enabled TVs were sold in 2013, and by 2015 these connected TVs will make up 55 percent of total TV sets, with an estimated 141 million sold globally.[4] According to Strategy Analytics, by 2017 nearly all mid- to high-end TV sets will include some form of IP connectivity either through the actual TV set or through devices such as Apple TV or Microsoft's Xbox.[5]

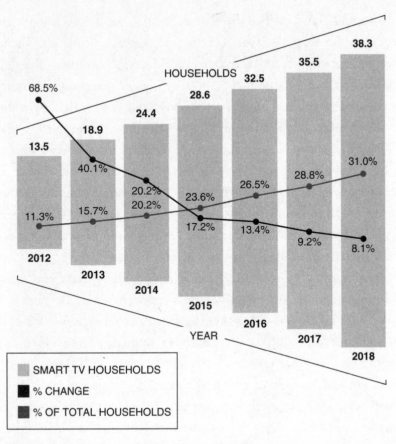

Figure 4.2 Growth in Smart TV Ownership in the USA.
Source: Emarketer, 2014.

As a consequence, everyone from Hulu in the United States to Sky in the united Kingdom and CCTV in China is laying the groundwork for adaptable TV advertising.

Adaptive TV advertising may perhaps take longer to scale than we think. Or maybe not. Only time will tell. In the meantime, let's take a closer look at why the adaptive layer of media is proving to be such a compelling proposition to marketers and why those in the foundational layer are enviously seeking ways to bring some of that digital magic dust into their world. For even within the adaptive layer there are two ends of the spectrum, one side increasingly dependent on technology, and the other side increasingly dependent on talent leveraging technology, and both extensively using real-time data (see Figure 4.3).

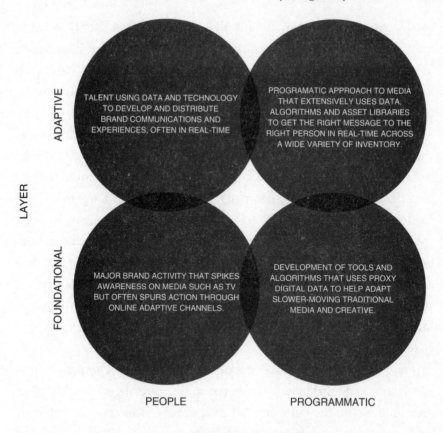

Figure 4.3 Different Adaptive Approaches to Different Types of Media.

The Magic of Cookies

Since the first online advertisement in 1994, the digital marketing industry has largely thrived on its ability to use a myriad of data sources to target specific audiences with specific messages. Most of this has historically been done by what is commonly called a "cookie", what many in the business consider the key building block of today's digital marketing. The term "cookie" is derived from "magic cookies," which was a computing technology name for the packet of data that a program sends back and forth. Now you know.

Today's cookies are basically a file that is put on your device and stores information about you and your online behavior and then transfers that information back and forth between your device and the Internet. Cookies can include all kinds of detailed data that essentially makes the Internet a more personalized and seamless experience. Without cookies you'd start your Internet experience from scratch each and every time, reentering user IDs, refilling shopping carts, and recustomizing pages ad nauseam.

For those of you who really want to know here is the explanation of the three primary types of cookies. The first type of cookie is normally from a brand's or publisher's website that you've visited and includes data that is specific to that company. Called first-party data, this information often includes your name, previous website behavior, your shopping basket, etc. In many countries, due to government regulations, you as a customer will need to opt in to have this cookie installed and thus essentially grant a company permission to keep this data on you stored. This is the best type of cookie information for marketers, but it is limited to those companies having a direct relationship with a customer, typically through their websites.

The second type of cookie data is essentially other company's first-party cookie data that can be shared and mixed together with other data sets. Again, the customer has to approve of this sharing, typically by opting in when registering or leaving details on a website. It's the next best thing after first-party data.

The third type of cookie is used for advertising, normally across publishers. This is called a third-party cookie, and it includes all types of granular data, such as your searches and website visits, and that data essentially determines what advertisements you might be interested in seeing. Third-party cookies can be extraordinarily detailed, but they always miss one vital piece of information: your identity. It may sound crazy, but this missing link forms the essential pact between advertisers and consumers. In effect, advertisers will collect data on you to send you better ads, but they will not intrude on your privacy by determining exactly who you are. Essentially, with third-party cookies you become an anonymous customer segment but with very particular interests and needs (see Figure 4.4).

This short and very simplified explanation of cookies is geeky but essential to understanding the magic of online marketing and its ability

Figure 4.4 Cookies Simplified.

to deliver highly adaptive advertising. For only digital advertising has the ability to intelligently combine cookie data with external variables, such as the weather or your physical location, to give marketers an unparalleled opportunity to adapt creative messages and media in real time. While digital advertising has some flaws and is far from perfect, it's a big step closer to the age-old marketing goal of getting the right message to the right person at the right place at the right time.

Now for the nontechies reading this book, all this talk about cookies, data, and algorithms can be complicated, which is why the industry has given it a nifty name: programmatic marketing. In a nutshell, programmatic marketing uses advanced technology to combine all this complicated stuff into a mostly automated tool that enables marketers to deliver adaptive advertising in a cost-effective manner. In effect, programmatic marketing is like taking your digital marketing from a Fiat to a Ferrari when it comes to sophistication in its ability to deliver precise results at high speeds.

Programmatic marketing is so compelling that eMarketer reports its share of digital media spend will grow by 50 percent over the next few years to roughly $53 billion in global media spend by 2018.[6] And eventually programmatic marketing will extend into other media, such as TV, and change the foundational layer of advertising. That change in TV is very small at the moment; according to Strategy Analytics, programmatic TV buying in the United States makes up less than 1 percent of total media spend at the moment.[7] However, that figure could climb to as much as 20 percent by 2018 if the digital TV media ecosystem continues to advance.

Some cable TV providers are doing everything they can do make programmatic marketing a reality. British cable TV provider Sky launched a new programmatic ad service called AdSmart in 2014. The AdSmart system uses cable TV's version of a first-party cookie—your subscription and viewing data—and combines that information with other data sources such as customer profiling company Experian to provide brands with thousands of different customer segments to target with multiple ad variations. These customer segments can get pretty specific, including whether or not you have a dog or cat and where you like to travel. As you watch a TV program, the system will intelligently deploy the right advertisement to the right household based on all of the accumulated data.

So does programmatic marketing work? The answer depends on how you use it. If you drive a Ferrari like a Fiat, the benefits are negligible. However, if you drive a Ferrari as it should be treated, with the proper fuel, data interpretation, and speed, then the benefits can be enormous.

Travel companies such as Lufthansa airlines have benefited greatly from programmatic marketing when it comes to targeting people exploring potential vacations and flights. Lufthansa's marketing team will leverage all types of cookie data to track search activity, your current location, and tourist sites you may have visited. For example, if you have searched on "warm weather holidays," live in "Munich," and have visited the official Bali Tourism website, you may very well receive a special Lufthansa promotion on its Munich to Bali daily long-haul flight. If you don't respond to this ad, Lufthansa may suggest an alternative promotion, say, from Munich to Phuket. Lufthansa could also add some additional external data to its targeting. For example, similar to the Cidre outdoor ad example, Lufthansa could decide to serve ads only when the weather outside is rainy or cold, when you are arguably most likely to be tempted to book a flight to a warmer destination. There are a myriad of other data variables that can be used to further refine Lufthansa's targeting. However, during this entire time Lufthansa doesn't have one very important data point: your identity. Lufthansa doesn't know exactly who you are, it just understands your potential interests from your online behavior.

Programmatic marketing seems intuitive for brands used to direct response marketing, but what about those marketers focused on brand-building metrics, such as awareness and message association? The answer seems to be the same. Programmatic marketing and data are fundamental to marketers grappling with the increasing importance of the adaptive layer.

Keith Weed, Chief Marketing and Communications Officer of the global consumer goods company Unilever, believes programmatic marketing is fundamental. "Digital and data use context to boost content, particularly on mobile. We can now use programmatic technology to target someone with a Magnum ice cream but only on a hot day and in the afternoon between 3:00 p.m. and 5:00 p.m. when we know they tend to be hungry. We can even use geo-location technology to help them to get to a local shop."[8] Luis Di Como, Unilever's Senior Vice President of Global Media, concurs. "Data is completely changing the way we approach media, in particular via programmatic, where we use technology and data to target the right people in the right place."[9]

When the top marketing brass at one of the world's leading consumer goods companies start singing the praises of data and programmatic marketing, you know it's time for the advertising industry to take notice.

Top Tips for Building a Programmatic Solution

1. Assess your options carefully. The industry is littered with programmatic solutions ranging from Google to small start-ups, each with different business models and pros and cons. Analyze each carefully and be aware that the industry is ripe for consolidation; not every solution will still be around in a few years.

2. Decide on the best model for your company. As part of your assessment determine the role your organization will play in programmatic marketing. Some clients, such as P&G, have taken programmatic in-house; others, such as Unilever, are cobuilding a capability with their agencies, and still others are completely outsourcing programmatic marketing.

3. Drive it like a Ferrari. Regardless of the model you choose, make sure you are inputting the data, intelligence, and creative assets that programmatic marketing requires to be truly successful. The more you put into the technology, the more you get out of it.

4. Don't forget the inventory. Arguably the biggest weakness in programmatic marketing is poor media inventory, which normally comes with poor ad verification, visibility, and brand safety. Explore premium inventory pools and ensure your brand is protected.

5. You still need people. While programmatic marketing brings a high level of automation to your digital marketing, it still requires actual people to make it really hum. In short, you still need a driver to drive the Ferrari, and normally that driver isn't someone used to driving a Fiat. You may need to upskill your talent along with your technology.

The Other End of the Adaptive Layer

The adaptive layer of advertising is also blessed with multiple always-on platforms that thrive on a steady stream of consumers and content.

This portion of the adaptive layer includes everything from Google search to your Facebook newsfeed. These destinations are frequented by millions of people on a daily basis and can be used by adaptive marketers to quickly change advertising based on any number of circumstances. In many respects this area of the adaptive advertising layer is more dependent on people. Certainly data and technology play a key role, but it's ultimately people who must observe the data and make decisions, either creatively or from a media perspective, who determine what to do, frequently in tandem with the foundational layer.

A great illustration of this happens every year during big events like the Superbowl or the Academy Awards, the Oscars. Big brands spend a fortune on developing and running a TV spot during these high-profile occasions and then use digital channels to proactively or reactively adapt their presence online to reflect the latest information flowing into their mission control centers.

Nabisco's Oreo brand arguably set the precedent for this type of advertising with its #dunkinthedark power-outage tweet during the 2013 Superbowl. Since then numerous other brands have followed in Oreo's footsteps. Samsung famously hijacked the 2014 Oscars when host Ellen DeGeneres tweeted a celebrity-packed selfie during the live broadcast with a Samsung phone. Ellen's tweet was retweeted over three million times, outdoing the previous retweet record holder, President Obama, by over two million.

Three interesting lessons emerged from the Oscar selfie. First, it later turned out that while Ellen's tweet looked spontaneous, it was actually part of a carefully crafted plan by Samsung as part of its rumored $20 million overall sponsorship and product placement deal with the Oscars. The lesson: Adaptive advertising still often requires some level of planning coupled with paid advertising, frequently in the foundational layer, to succeed. At the most basic level this advance planning could be the overarching framework within which spontaneous brand acts can occur, similar to the social guidelines encouraged in the preceding chapter.

The second lesson was the impact this digital tweet had on the broader public. While a large but still limited number of people saw the actual tweet, millions more heard about it on the news on TV, in the newspapers, and on the radio. The point here is that if done well, our highly adaptive layer of advertising can reverberate well beyond its digital roots, often in what we would consider the foundational layer of media, such as TV.

Finally, the third lesson is that adaptive messaging that leads with a broader social aspect rather than just the brand seems to resonate with a wider audience, something Kimberly-Clark's Chris Whalen identified as a key learning with Huggies. The Oreo's #dunkinthedark tweet was retweeted a mere 15,000 times compared to the Oscar selfie's three million, which wasn't immediately identified as a Samsung ad until later on. In fact, the most successful example of 2014 in this people-based portion of the adaptive layer was for a broader social cause, the Amyotrophic Lateral Sclerosis (ALS) #icebucketchallenge, which saw millions of people around the world dump a bucket of ice over their head, film it, and challenge others to donate to the charity or take the challenge themselves. Data and technology helped spread the word and keep the ALS team informed of the success of the program, but ultimately it was talent that came up with the idea and used a combination of social and online video channels to spread the word and the often hilarious videos, all for a very serious and worthy cause. Many people, including George Bush and Bill Gates, took the challenge, which ultimately led to over $100 million in donations to the ALS Association by the end of 2014 compared to the roughly $3 million that was donated the year before.

Google search may not appear to be the most creative of spaces, but it is yet another key component of the adaptive layer that companies can use to respond in real time. For example, the marketers of the Mars company's Snickers brand were looking for clever ways to bring their "You're Not You When You're Hungry" campaign to life online. The marketing team worked with Google to identify the most common misspelled search terms and then bought those terms on the premise that if you couldn't type correctly, perhaps you needed a Snickers bar as obviously you were not being you due to hunger. Now, not every search campaign will lend itself to this sort of creativity. However, Google does offer an opportunity for marketers to keep adapting and refining the searches they want their brand associated with as consumers' interests and needs change based on news, fashion, or other influencing factors.

The one thing that most marketers make clear is that this agile, people-based end of the spectrum doesn't replace the core foundational brand building that large, successful brands accomplish over time. It is this balance between a fast-moving digital world and the longer process of traditional advertising that can cause tension, when in reality the two mostly work together. As GroupM Chief Digital Officer Rob Norman states, "The utopian vision of data is that this information provides insights that unlocks creativity. It's a liberating force. The dystopian view is that it creates sets of judgments that are too instant rather than built over time, which conflicts with and challenges the patience that you need to build brands over the long term."

Over time this tension will work itself out as marketers develop a much more precise model for balancing these two adaptive and foundational layers even while they gradually merge. In the meantime, the adaptive layer gives advertisers a unique opportunity to use data and technology to think creatively and respond to events in real time.

Top Tips for People and the Adaptive Layer

1. Adapting can actually take more than one person. A quick response in real-time environments often requires a cross-functional team working together, and that applies even more so during high-profile events. Media, PR, creative message, technology and even the legal department need to collaborate to move fast.
2. Establish the guardrails or guidelines. Ensure the team understands the guidelines that define what they can and cannot do in real-time situations. Clearly indicate the parameters in areas such as creative freedom, budgets, and media choices.
3. Budget for adaptive marketing. Make sure your campaigns and initiatives have a budget sufficient to allow some ongoing adaptability, particularly for unforeseen events that offer unique opportunities.

4. Lead with the broader context. Some of the most successful campaigns on networks such as Facebook and Twitter see brands taking a backseat to a larger cultural or social event. Even in Google search brands should explore their broader keyword territory. Don't let the brand get lost, but at the same time don't let it get in the way. Think of the brand's broader relevance.

5. Leverage the foundational layer. TV is not the enemy of the adaptive layer. In fact the two layers can work together to create a bigger overall impact. Seek ways to leverage your foundational investment, particularly during events and occasions relevant to the brand and its target audience.

Connecting the Layers

According to the United Kingdom's Thinkbox and GroupM's Mediacom, 20 percent of total consumer response to a TV campaign in the United Kingdom happens on the Internet within ten minutes of exposure.[10] This data is just one of many stats proving that our adaptive and foundational layers are perhaps more connected than we realize. For many marketers, this connectivity through consumers sequentially or simultaneously bouncing between screens is either a headache or an unprecedented opportunity to adapt brand communications, both their creative message and media. In effect, how do you manage highly adaptive *consumers*, who follow their own rules rather than sticking with the old linear advertising journeys of the past?

One professor at Harvard did a comprehensive study on what tactics in a TV advertisement led to subsequent online engagement. Thales Teixeira and his team matched TV advertising data with website visits and online purchases from a 100,000 person panel on a second-by-second basis.[11] The research covered five industries, including apparel, telecom, travel, pizza, and online services and content. A variety of TV tactics and variables were considered including calls to action, such as encouragement to search or visit a social network; imagery used; and emotion versus product advertising.

The research showed some interesting results. For instance, no single advertising type could increase the number of website visits *and* online purchases among the multiscreeners participating. However, action-oriented ads were best for quickly driving people online, and the clearer the call to action given to consumers, the better the online results. Emotional and product ads led to an increase in online purchases, but without a visit to the website. Teixera's hypothesis was that the more emotionally and visually appealing a TV ad was, the less likely it was for someone to switch to another screen. In essence, for the moment at least, people were captivated by what was on the screen in front of them.

One way to try and solve the unpredictability of adaptive consumers is by leading them on a preferred journey rather than leaving that journey to chance. By mapping out various consumer journey scenarios, marketers can begin to connect the dots for specific target audiences, changing calls to action, messaging, even content to encourage fickle consumers to take that one additional step with the brand to deeper engagement.

Companies like Nestlé and American Express have codified the learning from hundreds of campaigns to give their marketing teams clear guidance on these tactics, in essence telling them what types of calls to action work best under what circumstances. GroupM's Rob Norman believes these simple but powerful mechanics can shift ROI. "We have demonstrable proof through rigorous testing that by adding a logical call to action, consumers will take that logical next step, leading to deeper engagement with the brand."

The following chart provides an example of how adaptive marketers are exploring the uses of various connection tactics, whether via simple calls to action on their advertising or via more advanced technologies, typically mobile applications. Which ones are ultimately selected will depend on your unique combination of brand, market, and target audience, particularly given the widely different penetration levels and usage of some mobile technologies. For example, QR (Quick Response) codes have failed to really take off in the United States and Europe. However, in China, QR codes have become a widely successful connecting tactic, particularly when it comes to purchasing items via mobile phones. The primary impetus has been the leading mobile social network WeChat, which has done such a great job of integrating the QR code reader technology into its mobile application. The lesson: You will have to be adaptive when it comes to the use of different techniques to connect the foundational and adaptive layers of your advertising. One size doesn't fit all (see Figure 4.5).

Top Tips for Connecting the Foundational and Adaptive Layers

1. Understand your customers. What is their consumption of either foundational or adaptive media throughout their journey, and how does it change? What are their key emotional or functional needs at each stage?

2. Determine how best to connect the two layers. How are your customers currently multiscreening between the two layers? What simple calls to action or more advanced technologies (for example, Shazam and Blippar) are available?

3. Ensure that you are making the right bets on new technology. Is the connective mobile app you selected widely used by your target audience? What are the barriers to using it? Is it easy to use? Does it have scale?

4. Test and learn. Which calls to action and technologies are generating the best connections? Have you A/B tested various combinations?

5. Anticipate more media going into the adaptive layer. Are you anticipating a greater shift to adaptive media either because more consumers are spending time there or because the foundational layer is being plugged into the Internet?

The Power of Proxy Data

Adaptive marketers can do more than just lead consumers from off-line foundational advertising to online adaptive destinations. In fact, the adaptive layer of advertising is giving marketers a wealth of information on how well their foundational layer of advertising is working. For example, via specific calls to action to visit Google or Twitter, you can measure

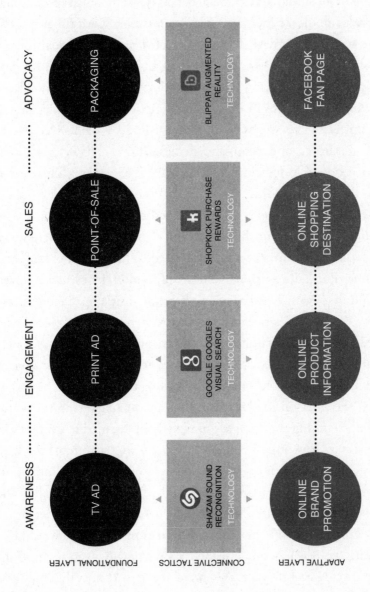

Figure 4.5 Different Ways to Connect Media Throughout the Consumer Journey.

whether a TV spot or media placement is driving searches on Google or generating significant social chatter. Marketers can then adjust their TV plan to upweight media placements or particular television spots that are generating more online activity. Such data is typically called "proxy data" as it provides an inexact but fairly decent measure of performance.

While much proxy data derives from off-line foundational calls to action, it's not the only source of inexact but extremely helpful data that has a known correlation to a result. For example, Kimberly-Clark's Kleenex marketing team in the United Kingdom used Google search data on flu-related keywords to adapt its off-line TV plan. Every week, Kleenex monitored and geo-mapped these flu-related Google search terms to geographic locations in the United Kingdom. This search data was then used to adjust the TV media schedule by moving media investment to areas in the UK where, based on the Google data, a flu outbreak was about to hit the population. For example, if there was a growing volume of searches with flu-related terms in Manchester and at the same time a diminishing volume in London, investment moved from London to Manchester. The result was an over 40 percent increase in year-on-year Kleenex sales adding up to a hefty 432,499 extra boxes sold. This is a simple example of how just one piece of data, Google search information in this case, can be used to adapt off-line media.

Some of the more cynical marketers reading this book may be shrugging their shoulders in the knowledge that many markets in the world have a long-standing tradition of annually booking media inventory in order to secure discounts. The United States is one such market where broadcasters and advertisers gather together every year to hammer out deals amid glamorous parties. In the United States this is called the "upfronts," and clients are often locked into a very unadaptive long-term commitment to TV inventory. While most marketers would like to replicate the Kleenex models, some may struggle given the upfront model, particularly if they are keen on securing discounts that may add more to ROI than an adaptive approach to TV. Fortunately, some marketers can have their cake and eat it too. Just ask President Obama.

The 2012 Obama reelection campaign used typical upfront tactics to secure discounted TV media inventory, but then adapted the creative and

TV spots based on real-time events, social bounces, and other inputs and proxy metrics. Therefore while the media wasn't adaptive—what the campaign managers bought is what they bought—the actual advertisement that appeared on the day, time, location, and channel varied depending on incoming data. A key message resonating with voters in Ohio was turned into a TV spot running in Ohio. Furthermore, different audiences in Ohio were targeted with slightly different versions of that TV spot depending on time of day or association with particular TV programs. In fact, the existing TV creative message was constantly monitored and adapted by Obama's team, and new content was quickly generated to capitalize on trending themes and topics as the campaign evolved.

While your ability to adapt off-line media is primarily dependent on market factors, it shouldn't stop you from exploring options. Even in the more extreme upfront markets it's possible to push for greater levels of adaptability as witnessed by the Obama 2012 campaign. As Obama himself would say: Yes, you can.

Top Tips for Adapting the Foundational Layer

1. Look for direct or proxy data to measure success. What real-time data is available to help you judge success in the foundational layer (e.g., searches from a TV spot, Likes on Facebook, mobile app downloads)? How can that adaptive data be used to inform changes in the foundational layer?

2. Explore portfolio approaches. Are there opportunities within your company or with partnerships to adapt who gets what air time based on ROI analysis and evolving situations? If your upfront investment is fixed, can you at least adapt what goes into that investment?

3. Develop different creative messages. Like Obama, can you adapt your creative message and advertising to improve ROI? Can you constantly adapt what message appears in front of what audience based on proxy metrics?

4. Buy cross-media packages. Are you pushing cross-media publishers, such as Conde Nast, to provide some level of flexibility

between their foundational and adaptive layers? Can they provide more adaptive layer opportunities based on the functional layer's performance?

5. Explore the boundaries of the foundational layer. Are there opportunities to test elements of the foundational layer that are being plugged into the Internet?

Pancakes and Pianos

Did you know that people who say they are "much shorter" than others are 50 percent more likely to say they have trouble falling asleep every night or most nights? Or that people who are "super fans" of Indian and Thai cuisine have the highest rates of having Twitter accounts compared to fans of other cuisines? Maybe you were already aware that people who love Ellen DeGeneres are more than twice as likely to love eating at the International House of Pancakes (IHOP) than those who don't like her. Too bad for IHOP that she's busy tweeting selfies for Samsung at the Oscars.

These are just a few of the gems that CivicScience's InsightStore has discovered as it has trawled the Internet for consumer insights derived from actual online data and over 27 million anonymous respondents who opted in.[12] This is the type of data and information that many marketers are increasingly seeking and exploiting in their desire to come up with better advertising.

Nestlé is one such leading marketer that has taken a very rigorous approach to applying such real-time insights to its bespoke communications planning process called "Brand Building the Nestlé Way." Nestlé's marketers are using the Internet as one giant focus group to test the effectiveness of everything from a creative tag line to which online video to run on television. Nestlé's Pete Blackshaw is unequivocal when it comes to the importance of using data and consumer insight for building relevance: "Digital and social media introduce a system of 'debits' and 'credits' to brand storytelling, and in the process hold us more accountable to brand fundamentals."[13]

Despite such claims, many in the advertising industry have long argued that data cannot replace creativity and that all this talk of data is actually detrimental to good old-fashioned creative work. The Cannes Lions International Festival of Creativity, the advertising industry's major annual gathering, is full of prominent creative directors trash-talking data scientists and anything related to data as if it were some scourge that had descended on creative departments around the world.

In reality, the answer is not binary. Marketers shouldn't be forced to choose one or the other. In fact, data and creativity can co-exist, complementing and supporting each other, and as with media, your place on the adaptive advertising spectrum determines exactly how they best come together.

For example, data can provide powerful customer insights that can better inform the creative brief. All of the implicit and explicit behavioral data from programmatic marketing gives communications planners a smorgasbord of insights on real people and their real behavior, rather than the esoteric waffling that often comes from customer focus groups and interviews. Data from monitoring the social buzz and search trend data can also provide great input for a creative brief and a content strategy as well as for the media strategy. Why would any marketer plowing a multimillion dollar budget into a prime-time TV spot not try and capture as much data and insight as possible for the creative briefing process?

As Unilever's Keith Weed says, "You need both data and creativity to really work together. You can be as creative as you like, but if you put the wrong content in front of the wrong audience it's a moot point."

One example cited by Weed is the use of Google search trends data to inform Unilever's content strategy. Recognizing that its teenage girl target audience simply adores YouTube, Unilever decided to partner with some of YouTube's user celebrities to create a new channel called "All Things Hair." The channel offers girls tips on the latest hairstyle trends and, of course, promotes Unilever hair care products, such as TRESemme, and even allow girls to purchase some products online. But how to identify the trends? What video content to produce? Unilever used Google search data to geolocate specific trends, questions, and discussions related to girls' hairstyles in specific parts of the United Kingdom. Search trends with a critical mass were then used to brief the content development team, whose members promptly created related videos to feature on the YouTube channel. "All Things Hair" is a great example of using real-time online data, in this case just from one source, to inform the creative and content strategy.

LA-based AdGreetz is taking adaptive video one step further by enabling marketers to leverage any type of data, including social, brand, third-party, geo/browser, and user-generated data, so as to produce and deploy relevant, personalized video messages on 15 channels, including e-mail, social, web, print, premium video, and banner ads. For example, the marketers of Oreo cookies developed a personalized birthday greeting from country/rock band Lady Antebellum in conjunction with Oreo's 100th birthday. The video features the band casually playing the piano while personally wishing you a happy birthday by name. It's a highly impactful way of mixing celebrity sponsorships and endorsements with the hyper-targeting and adaptive power of the Internet.

AdGreetz can help marketers personalize up to 1,250 different first names, roughly 80 percent of all first names in the United States. On-air talent records those names or other personalized data via short, separate close-up videos, which can then be edited and added to the beginning of a general video advertisement. Eric Frankel, founder and CEO of AdGreetz, says: "Traditional advertising builds awareness. What we do is adapt and personalize that commercial, creating up to 150,000,000 different variations."[14]

Studies suggest that people respond to these personal ads (see Figure 4.6). According to ChoiceStream, e-mails with personalized subject lines are 22 percent more likely to be opened, and 35 percent of Internet users in the United States said they would welcome more personalized ads or recommendations online.[15] AdGreetz's numbers back that up. According to Frankel, response rates from AdGreetz's personalized messages generate 50 percent to 250 percent more engagement and activation.

The work of AdGreetz may be just the tip of the iceberg when it comes to adaptive creative experiences. At the far end of the adaptive layer, marketers are already assembling the actual creative advertisement on the fly based on various real-time data points. Unilever experimented

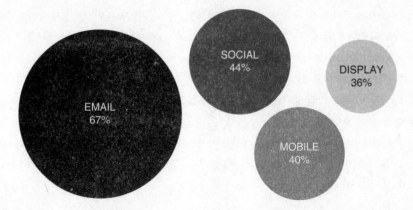

Figure 4.6   US Internet Users Who Think Digital Ad Personalization is Important, By Format.

Source: Responsys Survey Conducted by Ipsos Observer Cited in Company Blog, July 23, 2013.

with dynamic creative units for its Dove Men+Care campaign, essentially mixing Rugby Six Nations Championship news into the brand advertisements on the fly using Sizmek ad serving technology. The result was a 0.84 percent click-through rate, a rate significantly higher than the industry average, which generally hovers around 0.10 percent.

Dynamic creative is a bit like Iron Man's superhero suit he puts on as he prepares to go into battle. Various bits and pieces of the armor get assembled on the fly, depending on Tony Stark's specific situation and needs at any given time. With dynamic creative, the suit consists instead of various bits of the creative messaging rather than of body armor; it includes the imagery, the main message, even the specific product SKU, and all are combined based on the algorithm prediction on the optimal combination to get a certain result. Even TV is getting into the act. Advanced addressable TV targeting company Visible World uses a customer's cable TV box to create customized TV spots. All this is proof that the adaptive advertising spectrum is becoming more adaptive, regardless of what your creative director might say.

In this chapter we explored the full adaptive advertising spectrum, everything from programmatic marketing to agile marketing in the adaptive layer, to ways to bring greater flexibility and creativity to the foundational layer via greater use of proxy data. What should be clear from the examples is that data can support creativity in any part of the spectrum, whether simply feeding into the consumer insights for the creative brief or personalizing e-mails from celebrities (see Figure 4.7). For adaptive marketers there is no choice between data and creativity, the two must increasingly work together. As GroupM's Rob Norman puts it bluntly: "If you want to be adaptive, you have to be adaptively creative as well."

In our next chapter we will explore how leading adaptive marketers are leveraging real-time data to create a more compelling retail experience both online and off-line.

	LISTEN	ENGAGE	CUSTOMIZE
APPROACH	Use real-time data to inform your creative, content strategy, and media plans.	Use digital technology and platforms to engage with audiences in real-time.	Use data to create an adaptive brand experience or a systemized approach to advertising.
LEADER	Nestle, Unilever, Kimberly-Clark	Mondelez, Samsung	Unilever, Nestle
PRO'S	Captures real people and their real behaviours to help come up with better content and better distribution.	If done properly enables the brand to gain real relevance, reach and ROI.	Real-time adaption of the creative experience can significantly increase relevance and cut through the clutter.
CON'S	Takes time and effort to set-up the technology and ensure the data is statistically significant.	Often requires a foundational layer investment, and doesn't always equate to big numbers.	For programmatic, it requires data and technology. For other opportunities, it requires imagination.

Figure 4.7 Different Adaptive Approaches to Advertising.

Top Tips for Using Data to Improve Advertising

1. Codify your adaptive efforts via programmatic marketing. Combine all your data, algorithms, creative assets, and knowledge and institutionalize all this via a programmatic solution. Programmatic marketing is ultimately poised to make up a huge chunk of digital advertising, and you had best prepare for it.

2. Explore agile opportunities. At the other end of the adaptive layer, explore opportunities for the brand to have quick relevance through dynamic destinations like Facebook, Twitter, and Google.

3. Don't forget about the foundational layer. Brand building can be a long-term endeavor. Don't neglect the foundational building blocks and look for ways to build in some adaptability into what may appear to be inflexible at first.

4. Connect the adaptive and foundational layers. Consumers don't treat them as silos, neither should you. Explore ways to connect them via calls to action or new technologies. Leverage direct and proxy data to make them both work better.

5. Data and creative elements complement each other. Don't let anyone convince you otherwise. Whether informing the creative concept, adapting the experience in real time, or simply improving distribution, data is creative marketers' best friend.

CHAPTER 4.1

The Programmatic Solution on Data

Caspar Schlickum

CEO Europe, Middle East, Africa

Xaxis

Programmatic marketing (and its associated list of acronyms) is such a big buzzword now, that it has almost entered into everyday use for marketers. This comes with some responsibility, especially for practitioners. It's too easy to just throw some words around, make it sound complicated, and sit back to watch how people react.

The reality, though, is that as the word has matured, so have the "ad-tech" and "mar-tech" industries that support the application of programmatic technologies to marketing problems and opportunities.

But to really understand the nature of that evolution, it pays to think about what the actual benefit of programmatic marketing is. After all, all of this technology surely is a means to an end, rather than an end unto itself. And here the promise lies in better targeting, measurement, and engagement, and all of this adds up to ads that are much more relevant to consumers. The CMO council recently published a survey that showed that 63 percent of marketers see better targeting as the way to make marketing as a discipline relevant in their organizations (for the record, localization came second at 38 percent—quite a gap!)

Programmatic technology is really all about delivering the right ad to the right person and at the right time. Therefore, it's no big surprise that the industry has matured to meet the evolving needs and levels of understanding of the advertising industry. This evolution has created what we could choose to think of as Programmatic 2.0 (OK, that's a huge simplification—this is a fast-moving world and depending on how we're counting we might well be at 3.0, or 4.0!)

Programmatic 1.0 was about real-time buying. An abundance of (cheap and low-quality) inventory drove certain pricing and market dynamics. Marketing was an industry dominated by technology and characterized by a lack of data (yes, big data was a big buzz word then too, but very few players were actually using it). As such, unless you just wanted to access lots of very cheap inventory, programmatic was not really adding much value.

Programmatic 2.0, on the other hand, is much more sophisticated. Data is king, and smart clients, publishers, and agencies are working on data strategies that not only protect the value of the data, but are interoperable. Extensibility of data across platforms, devices, and media is key.

In addition, there is a renewed focus on execution, a recognition that the application of programmatic technology to trading (via real-time bidding or RTB) actually makes many age-old industry problems worse, not better (for example, fraud and viewability). As such, Programmatic 2.0 is governed by very different market dynamics, a market with a scarce supply of quality inventory and where trading relationships and scale still matter.

At the same time analytics is becoming increasingly important in helping marketers understand exactly how this data and technology can solve real marketing problems (i.e., sales and brand equity). And that's where the ongoing evolution of programmatic becomes so interesting for clients who are adapting their marketing strategies in real time. This new data-fuelled world, where programmatic technologies are about so much more than cheap reach, means that the investment in CRM, the time spent understanding the media environment, and the investment in analytics is *more* important and exciting today than it was before and certainly more valuable than it was with Programmatic 1.0.

CHAPTER 5

Blurred Lines

I n the preceding chapters we've seen many examples of adaptive marketers using real-time data to develop better products and experiences, enhance customer service, and improve advertising. However, the use of data doesn't stop there. In fact, real-time data can be used to gain competitive advantage in arguably the most important part of the consumer journey: the actual purchase of a product or service. This chapter explores how adaptive marketers are exploiting real-time data to adapt both online and off-line commerce. In fact, the line between these two is increasingly becoming blurry as shoppers get more sophisticated in *their* use of data and technology.

Take Me Out to/of the Ball Game

What ticket price would you be willing to pay to go to a professional baseball game even if it was raining? How much more would you spend to see an all-star pitcher take the mound? Does loyalty to your favorite baseball team have a cost? The St. Louis Cardinals professional baseball team thinks it knows the answers to each of these questions and more.

The Cardinals are one of many professional sporting teams in the United States that are dynamically adapting the ticket price to specific games in real time based on data that is fed into carefully constructed algorithms. These algorithms have codified the Cardinals' years of experience in understanding exactly how different variables impact expected demand for a particular game and the price that a fan would be willing to pay for a ticket.

So exactly what data goes into these secret algorithms?

The Cardinals look at a variety of third-party data sources and exogenous factors. For example, weather forecasts and roster changes are key elements. For example, if an upcoming Saturday afternoon baseball game is due to have sunny weather and include an all-star pitcher, then the ticket prices go up. Alternatively, a dull cloudy day at the end of the rotation means lower prices. The Cardinals continue to adapt the prices all the way up to game time to reflect any new real-time data that suggests a change in potential demand. The only exception is the ultraloyal season ticket holder who is immune from such variances: rain or shine, the price remains the same.

Another interesting twist to the system is the marketing component. When the Cardinals drop prices, they don't do so in a vacuum. Many price drops are tied to a new concept the Cardinals call Dynamic Deals, which are powered by a company called Qcue started by CEO Barry Kahn. These adaptive prices are highlighted for anyone looking to buy Cardinals tickets and advertised during broadcasts as one of the best values in the stadium. According to Kahn, "Communication and transparency of a pricing strategy is incredibly important. It is not only what distinguishes a successful strategy like the Cardinals' from a public relations failure like the ones we have seen from Amazon, but it also drives sales when prices are dropped. If a price is dropped and nobody knows, will it create additional sales?"[1]

Has this new adaptive pricing model delivered results? According to the Cardinals, this dynamically priced ticket model has delivered greater benefits for the team's fans and for the company. For example, in 2013 alone, 53 percent of the Cardinals' games had tickets available for $10 or less, while 51 percent of games had tickets available for only $5. Under the old fixed-price model, 40 percent of seats ended up unsold while 10 percent of tickets across the industry were resold on the secondary market at an average of double the face value. Furthermore, the Cardinals now have much better information to price premium seats, which deliver higher profit margins for the company at a price the most fanatical of fans are willing to pay. In the end, with the new adaptive pricing model the net effect is fewer empty seats for both the Cardinals and their fans.

Qcue is providing a similar flexible pricing system to other sports teams, including those in basketball, football, and hockey. Qcue's Kahn believes the value exchange between consumer and company is clear: "Implementing a dynamic pricing strategy with clear objectives and fluid price changes allows teams to reclaim millions in revenue while being more creative in how they fill the stadium, putting fans in better seats and creating a better atmosphere in the venue." Qcue clients such as the Cardinals have used the company's software to make more than 1.6 million price changes and generate millions of dollars in incremental revenue.

Other businesses are experimenting with similar adaptive pricing models. Take Uber, the mobile app and highly disruptive transportation and taxi firm. Uber is testing what it calls surge pricing, which is a model that adjusts the prices of some of its cars in real time based on variables, such as the day and time, whether a big event is being held, and the weather. The result is a more expensive Uber ride if it's Friday after the theatre on a cold, rainy, evening. Alternatively, the price will drop if the opposite conditions prevail. Uber's pricing is still typically below that of the average taxi ride, but the company is experimenting with the price elasticity is does have within those parameters.

Pavlov and Pricing

The St. Louis Cardinals and Uber pricing models are just two examples of a nascent but rapidly developing form of adaptive marketing where real-time data is used to create better business outcomes by adjusting prices based on anticipated demand and existing supply.

Adaptive pricing isn't a new phenomenon. Airlines have been using similar models for many years; the industry introduced its SABRE computer booking system back in 1960, and ever since consumers are used to computers raising or dropping airline ticket prices based on multiple factors, such as remaining seats on a plane, the time of the year, or other mysterious but accepted variables. In fact, many consumers have taken it upon themselves to master these algorithms, studying patterns and identifying the optimal time to purchase a ticket. For those who want to know about this, a recent Cheapair.com study discovered the best time to buy an airplane ticket is seven weeks before departure date. The worst days were between 208 to 210 days before the flight.[2]

What has evolved over the years since the introduction of SABRE is the variety, volume, and speed of data sources that organizations can use to shape pricing strategies. In short, marketers have more instant information at their fingertips than ever before to establish the optimal price for target audiences and for the company to generate the best business results under certain conditions, which is sometimes of its own doing, sometimes outside of its control. Furthermore, marketers can increasingly change the price of those products and services in real time, particularly as more goods are sold online and as the supply and demand equilibrium changes. In a hyperconnected world, even a vending machine can instantly change its prices.

Take Limon&Nada, a popular soft drink brand in Spain and owned by Coca-Cola. Limon&Nada is particularly delicious when the weather warms up, but of course, Spaniards have many different options to quench their thirst on a hot day. Therefore, the Limon&Nada marketing team decided to break through the clutter by pricing a bottle based on the temperature. That is, whenever the mercury in the vending machines' virtual thermostat went up, the price of Limon&Nada went down, thus encouraging consumers to go get a discounted bottle whenever they break a sweat.

Limon&Nada's marketing team sought to develop a conditioned reflex, similar to the one developed by Russian scientist Ivan Pavlov in his experiments with dogs. A conditioned reflex is consistent instinctive behavior directly elicited by some sort of sensory stimuli—taste, touch, smell, sight, sound, etc. With Pavlov's dogs it was the ringing of a dinner bell; for Limon&Nada it was the first trickle of sweat on a customer's brow caused by soaring temperatures outside.

What's compelling about the Limon&Nada example is that the marketing team didn't use big data. As in so many adaptive marketing examples, the Limon&Nada team was able to find one single data source that had a proven impact on consumers' demand for their product: the temperature. One small piece of data, one very clever variation in pricing.

Let's look at another example. The Bull & Bear Steakhouse at the Waldorf-Astoria in New York City uses a similar single data point to determine pricing of its beverages. The Steakhouse bar gives a discount of $1 on cocktails for every 1 percent that the market declines during that day. The worse the market performs, the bigger the discount on your cocktail, all the way to a maximum of $5. Weary investors have thus developed a Pavlovian instinct to head to the Bull & Bear after a tough day of trading because they know they'll get a discount on their drinks. One small piece of data, one quick way to get a discount on your cocktail.

Sometimes these data points may not be so obvious to a customer. For example, the Swedish travel firm Orbitz uses proxy data for a person's income to adapt its recommendations when a person searches for hotels. Orbitz detects the user's mobile operating system and then suggests a cheaper hotel for Android and Windows users while Apple iOS customers get a more expensive recommendation. So if you are searching for a hotel in London, Android phone users will be recommended a Holiday Inn, while the Apple users will be suggested the Four Seasons. Why? According to the Orbitz marketing team, Apple users on average spend $20 to $30 more per night on hotels than their Android and Windows counterparts, a significant difference given that a hotel booking for one night is around $100. Apple users are also 40 percent more likely to book into a four- or five-star hotel than those using another operating system.[3]

One data point and one strong correlation to the price a consumer is willing to pay based on that variable.

Some Common Pricing Variables

1. Weather. Highly localized data, such as temperature and precipitation, can be used to determine anticipated demand and optimal pricing. Companies like the Weather Channel can provide

real-time weather feeds that can be plugged into your adaptive pricing models.

2. Location. Your exact location, either home or on the move, can be used to adapt pricing to encourage store visits or a quick online purchase. Most media networks offer either location detection or geolocation targeting ability with their advertising.

3. Device/Operating System. As shown by the Orbitz example, your operating system, device, installed applications, even your carrier can provide useful proxy data on your target audience to refine recommendations and pricing.

4. Health. A relatively new variable. Biometric and fitness-related data from health applications and devices can be used when allowed by a consumer to adjust promotions and pricing.

5. Behavior. An individual's behavior, including searches and visits to websites or applications can be used to refine pricing to close the sale.

Digital Price Discrimination

The Orbitz case differs slightly from the previous examples in one major way: the recommendation and pricing model is not readily transparent to the consumer. The individual searching for a hotel has no way of knowing that her operating system is directly impacting the price she will likely pay for a hotel room. It's in this increasingly opaque world of nontransparent adaptive pricing where marketers will need to carefully navigate the ethics regarding price discrimination. If different rules apply to different people, then negative emotions may be stirred up and such methods, in the worst case, may be breaking some laws.

Obviously, the practice of charging different prices to different customers has been around for ages and is largely legal as long as you stay within the government or industry guidelines. For example, one notable exception is that prices must never be altered based on an individual's race, sexual preference, or other characteristics that could be used to discriminate against people. In fact, this issue is serious enough that the government of the United States has passed legislation over the years, including the Sherman Antitrust Act and the Robinson-Patman Act, to provide clear rules regarding pricing models to avoid anticompetitiveness or discriminatory practices. Indeed, other countries and trade confederations, such as the European Union, have similar regulations in place. In the EU, price discrimination regulations cut across national boundaries and are designed to protect consumers from being charged different prices based on their nationality or place of residence in the European single market.

What has changed since much of this legislation was passed is the proliferation of new data that is now available to marketers via the Internet. On the positive side, marketers now have more information than ever before to align supply and demand. On the negative side, marketers can unwittingly end up using data that may be considered discriminatory, either directly or via proxy correlation. As with many things on the Internet, the lines are often blurred and unclear.

For example, according to a *Wall Street Journal* investigation, several large online office supply companies in the United States, such as Office Depot and Staples, were believed to be adapting the price on the same product based on the buyer's location. In effect, if you placed an order online, your physical location determined the price you would be charged by Office Depot on the same stapler: those in lower-income neighborhoods received a discounted price of $14.29 while those in more affluent neighborhoods were charged $15.79. Other factors, such as the proximity of a competitor's physical store also impacted the price; the closer a competitor's retail location to you, the lower the online price.[4]

Some, most likely including the aforementioned retailers, would argue this location-based pricing methodology is a simple online recreation of what retailers do in the real world; most companies will price goods based on local factors, whether using demand-oriented consumer data (e.g., local wealth, category interest) or supply-side considerations (real estate, transportation costs, competition, etc.).

However, cynics would argue that determining online prices based on location and local wealth data may be discriminatory. While consumers intuitively know that going to the Office Depot on the opposite side of town may result in some savings, it's unclear whether such practices would be acceptable online, where most people expect greater transparency and the same set of rules regardless of location. In fact, one of the great benefits of the Internet is to make location largely irrelevant: online you can buy anything from pretty much anywhere.

Consequently, while normative adaptive pricing models are accepted both off-line and online, e.g., discounts for loyalty or customer acquisition, changing online prices based on income or other demographic information is a more dangerous practice, one that could potentially backfire on a company if not handled properly. According to some recent Annenberg Public Policy Center research, 76 percent of Americans would be bothered to find out other people paid a lower price for the same product.[5] Consequently, any adaptive pricing model needs to be carefully evaluated to determine the level of transparency and the exact parameters and rules concerning data usage and application.

Despite some of these concerns, many companies have been successfully experimenting with such adaptive pricing models for years, largely without consumers' consent or knowledge and well within the parameters of industry best practice as well as government rules and regulations. Lingerie powerhouse Victoria's Secret was an early adopter of adapting pricing techniques. As early as 1996 Victoria's Secret mailed different versions of the same catalogue, with different prices offered for the same item to different groups of consumers. Through such basic adaptive techniques, Victoria's Secret created a real demand curve that assessed the willingness of different customer segments to pay different prices for the same goods, all before the Internet really caught on.

What about the granddaddy of online retailers? While Amazon's pricing model is largely shrouded in secrecy, it's clear from constant e-mails and other notifications that the price of those items sitting in your shopping basket or wish list seem to adapt over time. In fact, way back in 2000, media in the United States picked up on numerous customer complaints that Amazon was using dynamic pricing practices to adjust the cost of a DVD in real time supposedly based on predicted ability to pay calculated by analyzing many factors, including past purchase history and location. Amazon never revealed the details of the test. However, Amazon spokesman Bill Curry later stated that the tests were useful in determining a price point. Eventually, Amazon ended up refunding 6,896 angry customers an average of $3.10 each, or a total of $21,377.60, in order to quell the public outcry.[6] How the company actually approaches pricing remains largely a mystery to this day. The clear exception is Amazon's cloud-based service, which uses a bidding model to enable customers to buy computing and cloud-capacity in real time based on market dynamics, a practice more acceptable with nonstorable commodities.

Top Tips on Adaptive Pricing

1. Avoid discriminatory pricing models. Don't alter pricing based on fixed consumer characteristics such as age, sex, or ethnicity. This will only antagonize consumers if price differences become apparent and could lead to a lawsuit if the practice breaks market regulations.
2. Reward loyal customers. Offering discounts for consumers who regularly order from you will encourage repeat business and may increase bulk orders. It's a well-known and widely accepted practice.
3. Use exogenous variables. External data variables, such as the weather or time of the year, that affect everyone can be used to your advantage, especially for seasonal products, and they also provide a transparent guarantee that you are not discriminating against any particular group.
4. Use data generated online to guide differences in pricing. Assess anonymized website traffic and purchasing patterns to ascertain links between certain events and fluctuations in demand.
5. Run competitions. Randomly allocate discounts of differing percentages at set times. This can also be a good way of gauging how much your customers are willing to pay—and more important, this element of randomization avoids discrimination.

The Story of Sam Odio

How can adaptive marketers crack the code on dynamic pricing and promotion tactics to optimize conversion?

Fortunately, over the years as the Internet has matured and expanded, entire businesses have emerged in an attempt to help marketers navigate Amazon, Alibaba, and other ever-expanding and evolving e-commerce ecosystems. Sam Odio is one such adaptive pricing pioneer. Sam started Freshplum in 2011 to help marketers find ideal price points for specific products and specific audiences. The Freshplum team spent two years perfecting its algorithms, and now the team has a robust model in place that helps companies like L'Oréal adapt prices in real time.

Here's a relatively simple explanation of Freshplum. The company's technology essentially lets retailers embed some code on their own retail website, which activates an algorithm that can decide in real time whether to generate offers. This decision-making engine is Freshplum's secret sauce. It essentially assesses and profiles consumers when they visit the retailer's website, looking at nondiscriminatory variables such as consumers' history and propensity to purchase. Some of the data assessed includes how they go to the website, whether they are revisiting, their location, and the time of day. Based on this information, Freshplum's pricing algorithm determines whether these consumers are likely to spend with or without a discount. In the former scenario, Freshplum automatically serves up a promotion with a price reduction, thus saving the consumer some money and increasing the odds of the retailer converting the visit into a sale.

L'Oréal is one company that has successfully used Freshplum's technology. Like so many others in the cosmetics and beauty industry, the giant French company needed to balance the need to drive sales while maintaining brand equity. Freshplum integrated its proprietary technology into L'Oreal's Lancôme USA website, which includes a variety of tools to help returning and registered shoppers as well as window shoppers with no history or accounts. The Freshplum technology assessed all of this on-site behavior from various customers to develop marketing rules for various promotions that would best resonate with the visitors to LancômeUSA.com. All of this activity was measured using A/B testing and a control group not exposed to any of the Freshplum logic. The result was irrefutable: using real-time data, Freshplum increased conversion rates and revenue by 90 percent for Lancôme's new "indifferent" visitors by exposing them to the most effective offer. At the same time, Lancôme retained its cherished brand equity by avoiding the perils of couponing. Through these tests Lancôme also discovered several other variables that impacted the likelihood of conversion. For example, the weather had an impact on the probability of a window shopper making a purchase. Furthermore, the customer's browser also had an impact; visitors using certain web browsers were up to twice as likely to purchase. All of this information proved extraordinarily valuable as Lancôme and L'Oréal built out an adaptive pricing and communications model.

Companies like Freshplum will continue to grow if e-commerce forecasts are accurate (see Figure 5.1). According to eMarketer, over one

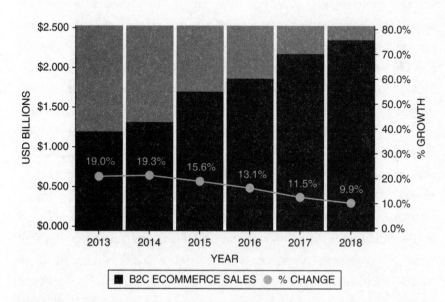

Figure 5.1 Forecasted Growth in e-Commerce Sales Worldwide.
Source: Emarketer, July 2014.

billion online users will spend more than $1.471 trillion in e-commerce purchases in 2014; this number doesn't even include B2B transactions. B2C e-commerce alone has grown by 20 percent year-on-year between 2013 and 2014 with continued growth projected over the next few years, which will led to $2.356 trillion in online sales by 2018.[7] These are some seriously big numbers. However, there's much more to the story than just online sales.

Blurred Lines #1

While e-commerce will continue to grow, it's important to remember that many people will still buy goods from physical stores. According to WPP's GroupM, even by 2018, roughly 90 percent of total sales will still take place in stores.[8] Consequently, it's critical for marketers to not lose sight of what's happening in the brick-and-mortar shops, where the lines between online commerce and physical shopping are rapidly blurring, mainly due to one device: the mobile phone.

In effect, mobile phones, particularly the smart kind, are becoming the ultimate shopping assistant used in a myriad of ways by consumers, sometimes in scenarios that can give marketers a competitive advantage, but in other cases can create potential threats. For example, according to the University of Southern California's Center for the Digital Future's 2013 Digital Future Report, 68 percent of millennial consumers in the United States have compared a price on their mobile phone; in contrast, only 43 percent of nonmillennial customers report doing the same.[9] The same report discovered that 46 percent of these mobile millennials looked for a better price nearby via their mobile phones, and 23 percent actually made a purchase via their mobile phone in the physical store (see Figure 5.2). All told, eMarketer estimates 124.8 million consumers aged 14 and over in the United States will shop with a smartphone device this year, a trend that will be reflected around the world and will surely expand as the number of mobile-wielding shoppers continues to grow. For instance, eMarketer projects the number of mobile shoppers will rise from 17.3 million in 2014 to 144.8 million; a figure that represents roughly 45 percent of

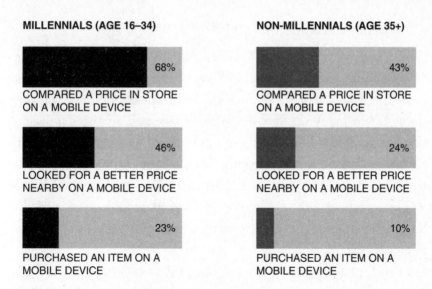

MILLENNIALS (AGE 16–34)

68%
COMPARED A PRICE IN STORE ON A MOBILE DEVICE

46%
LOOKED FOR A BETTER PRICE NEARBY ON A MOBILE DEVICE

23%
PURCHASED AN ITEM ON A MOBILE DEVICE

NON-MILLENNIALS (AGE 35+)

43%
COMPARED A PRICE IN STORE ON A MOBILE DEVICE

24%
LOOKED FOR A BETTER PRICE NEARBY ON A MOBILE DEVICE

10%
PURCHASED AN ITEM ON A MOBILE DEVICE

Figure 5.2   Growing Trend for Millennials to Use Mobile Phone When Shopping.
Source: Center for the Digital Future, USC, 2013 Digital Future Report.

the population of the United States and 74 percent of the total digital shopping population.[10]

Recent research also suggests that mobile phones are used for more than just comparing prices in physical shops. For example, Nielsen has discovered that nearly half of smartphone owners in the United States use shopping lists on their devices, and 49 percent say they've used mobile coupons via smartphones. Locating a store is the most likely activity among smartphone shoppers (76 percent), and reading reviews of recent/future purchases is the most common shopping activity among tablet owners (55 percent). After they make purchases, many mobile shoppers write reviews (23 percent of tablet shoppers) and comment on their purchases using social media (26 percent of smartphone shoppers).[11]

All the research and data leads to one key conclusion: mobile phones are currently playing and will continue to play a critical role all the way from the beginning of the physical shopping experience to potential postpurchase advocacy. Even while in-person sales at physical stores will continue to exceed e-commerce sales, mobile devices will enable companies to explore a myriad of adaptive marketing techniques in both spaces.

If You Can't Beat Them...

On a recent visit to Toys"R"Us I was able to save a not insignificant $27 by simply using my Amazon Price Check application to scan barcodes and find cheaper prices online. Such showrooming has become the norm in many people's shopping experiences. In these situations the consumer is looking for more information, even different pricing, on the goods in a store, sometimes looking in alternative online shops; this is a concern, to say the least, particularly for retailers who still rely on physical stores for the bulk of their sales, sales that have been fuelled by historically strong in-store conversion rates ranging from 95 percent in groceries to 20 percent in fashion.[12]

In fact, according to POPAI, 76 percent of purchase decisions are made at the point of sale.[13] While this is a blended data point that will vary by product category, the statistic does suggest that the probability of buying something in a physical store is higher than the online equivalent, where the shopping conversion rate is on average 3 percent.[14] Consequently, the challenge, and the opportunity, for many brands and retailers is to maintain or improve these physical conversion rates even with the increasing usage of smartphones by consumers who are flitting between the physical shopping experience and mobile applications.

The solution may follow the old adage "If you can't beat them, join them." If mobile technology is playing such an influential role, why not use it to your advantage rather than pretending mobile doesn't exist? Indeed, proactive use of mobile and adaptive strategies may be the most effective solution to counter competitors' alternatives readily available on your consumers' smartphone. For example, if you know that the length of the payment queue in a store may lead to abandonment, why not trigger some added pricing incentive or fast pass utility via the customer's mobile phone?

Starbucks is now letting its customers do just that because of one idea that was selected from MyStarbucksIdea.com, which was covered in chapter 2. This new service is being tried out in various US cities and is essentially an enhancement to the existing MyStarbucks mobile app. The new mobile feature allows customers to get a head start on their day by ordering their desired food and drinks ahead of time and prepaying so they can avoid the cash register altogether. By the time they get to their local Starbucks, their order is ready to be picked up.

The new Starbuck's feature is a simple solution to the showrooming phenomenon; use mobile technology in advance of the retail experience to avoid any later disintermediation. However, the Starbucks example is largely dependent on customers having the MyStarbucks app preinstalled on their phone, which raises one of the key complexities in using mobile to get your message in front of your customers.

Launching your own mobile application, as Starbucks has done, is one option albeit an extremely difficult one; there are over a million apps in the Apple iTunes store, and according to Nielsen, the average user has only 41 apps on his or her smartphone, with only 8 of them used every day. Consequently, becoming one of the chosen 41 or one of the magnificent 8 is a real challenge. Those eight apps make up, according to Nielsen, roughly 80 percent of US consumers' mobile browsing time; this number is even higher in markets such as China.[15] Consequently, marketers are presented with the stark reality that to even get seen on a mobile device, they need to somehow embed their app into the app ecosystem, perhaps not even as their own app but as an element of a more commonly used one. Fortunately, there are some viable options, which vary depending on location, target audience, and exact marketing ambitions.

Shopkick has emerged as one of the more popular of the emerging mobile shopping assistants. Essentially, consumers earn rewards and get special promotions, also known as "kicks," simply by walking into a retail store. These kicks can be redeemed for all kinds of things, including gift cards, free food, song downloads, even charity donations. Consumers seem to love these kicks. According the most recent publically available data from Shopkick, its users have earned $25 million and redeemed seven million gift cards since the application launched in 2010. In addition, users have scanned over 70 million products. To date, Shopkick users have viewed four billion product offers and walked into 35 million stores, which is why major retailers including

Target, Best Buy, and Macy's are all extensively using the application. For brands Shopkick provides an opportunity to partner with retailers to create dynamic promotions and experiences via a preinstalled mobile application already extensively used by consumers.

Shopkick is not alone in this. Dozens of other mobile shopping applications are also fighting to be one of your chosen 41 mobile applications. Each offer slightly different user benefits and business models. Punchcard helps retailers connect consumers to virtual loyalty cards via "punches" rather than kicks, while Swipely lets customers earn cash-back rewards whenever they use their credit or debit cards with any point-of-sale system in a store. China's WeChat has had enormous success in integrating shopping functionality directly into its mobile app via QR codes. With over 500 million users, WeChat is arguably the biggest shopping and social network hybrid app in the world, a fact not lost on Twitter and Facebook, who will surely continue to seek ways to build more e-commerce functionality into their applications.

Twitter has recently worked with both Amazon and American Express to integrate commerce functionality into its mobile app. Through the Amazon partnership, Twitter users can link their Amazon accounts to their Twitter handles. They will then be able to respond to links to Amazon products with the hashtag #AmazonCart to place the items automatically into their Amazon cart. Twitter has also worked with American Express to enable consumers to "sync" their credit card details with their Twitter handle to make purchases and get special promotions.

The telecom giant O2 offers another service in the United Kingdom called Priority Moments for small businesses. The program is bundled into O2's Priority Moments customer loyalty program and essentially gives customers unique promotions and deals in their area. It takes roughly three minutes for a local business to create an offer, which can be managed and adapted at any time. Over 17,000 small businesses in the United Kingdom are active in the program and generate a myriad of hypertargeted mobile adaptive promotions for O2 customers every day.

O2's Priority Moments is proof that brands can create a successful app. In fact, several retailers have managed to get a decent installed base for their mobile applications, which are typically virtual versions of existing customer loyalty programs that have been migrated and supercharged onto a customer's mobile phone. For example, Walmart's iPhone and Android application sends its users eGift cards if a local competitor is advertising a lower price. The app also recognizes when you are in physical store and naturally sends you store promotions and useful information. You can scan products, build customer shopping lists, and even refill prescriptions for quick pickup.

Mobile shopping apps can also be fun. Guatemalan shoe store Meat Pack "gamified" the shopping experience via a mobile app. During a short contest, consumers could download the brand's Hijack mobile application, which then used the phone's geolocation technology to detect when a possible customer had entered the proximity of the shopping mall where Meat Pack is located. Once identified, the customer was given a so-called discount clock on the app, which essentially gave the customer 100 seconds to get from his or her starting point in the mall to the Meat Pack store. The discount level started at 99 percent off the product price, with the amount you saved diminishing by 1 for every second. Thus the faster the person got into the store, the bigger the discount: if you made it into the store in 10 seconds, your discount level was 89 percent off the product price. If you made it in 60 seconds, you only got a 39 percent discount (99 minus 60), and so on. If you ran past 100 seconds, you were out of luck.

Meat Pack successfully used adaptive gaming techniques to generate footfall into the store, get customers to bypass their competitors in the mall, and give those consumers special adaptive prices based on their speed to the shop as clocked on the mobile application. More than 600 customers were hijacked during the competition. However, that number was small compared to the larger buzz generated by the content on social networks and in the news. By the way, Pedro Rodriguez got the record with an 89 percent discount.

For many brands and retailers, these mobile apps—whether their own or ones created through a partnership—provide a scaled means to drive footfall into physical stores via highly adaptive utilities, experiences, and promotions relevant to specific consumers based on profile, shopping history, and physical location.

Top Tips on Using Mobile Apps

1. Stress test your app. Do not just run off and create your own mobile application or keep pumping your efforts into an existing one that has largely failed. Getting onto your customer's mobile phone is a lot more difficult than you think.
2. Assess partnerships. If you come to the conclusion that you need to partner, assess the options on the market and which apps are most relevant to your customers and your brand ambitions.
3. Hedge your bets. There may be more than one mobile application worth exploring. Experiment and test your options, which will range from shopping assistants to loyalty apps.
4. Find the value exchange. Determine what customers really want from the mobile experience. Your options will range from utilities to improve the retail experience to adaptive promotions to fun brand experiences.
5. Convert your advertising into sales. Explore ways to better leverage your advertising footprint by enabling people to instantly buy products via their mobile phone.

Supercharging Retail

Some retailers are looking beyond mobile applications to enhance the retail experience. These companies are creating such compelling and personalized adaptive shopping experiences that conversion rates are holding steady and are even improving. Or the retail experience is so impactful that it is leaving a branded emotional residue that lingers long past the physical experience and leads to a digital or physical sale at a later date.

British retailer Burberry is one company that has fully embraced an adaptive retail experience supercharged with all types of advanced technology that encourages consumer engagement and in-store sales conversion. Burberry's 44,000 square foot store in London is a brick-and-mortar reflection of the brand's website and effortlessly blends the digital and physical brand experiences. RFID (radio-frequency identification), tiny little chips that can store and send information to other objects, are woven into all of the apparel, and this leads to an adaptive and customized experience featuring related products and accessories. Magic mirrors also feature video footage related to the clothes customers have selected, including fashion show runway footage and other exclusive content. In short, it's such a compelling experience that it pulls customers into the physical store through word of mouth.

Beacon technology is another buzzword popping up across the industry, but one worth paying attention to, particularly considering that inMarket, a beacon supplier company, conducted research that found that consumers receiving a beacon notification are ten times more likely to buy the advertised product than those who do not receive one.[16]

Beacons are essentially an enhanced version of Bluetooth wireless technology that enables communication for a distance of up to 164 feet, much more than today's Bluetooth, which only transmits for up to 32 feet, or even near field communication (NFC), which requires a physical tap to another device; that is, it essentially requires your mobile phone to physically interact with another machine. With beacon technology you can communicate with something else from a very long distance away, thus freeing up consumers from the physical constraints of NFC systems. Beacons are now automatically built into most smartphones, including any Apple iPhones starting with iOS7 or Android phones using the 4.4 (Kit Kat) operating system or above.

Some innovative companies have already experimented with beacons to create adaptive retail experiences. In the United Kingdom, downtown London is being transformed into one giant beacon experiment and experience. Retailers like Hamleys, Armani, Longchamp, and Hackett have installed beacons in their Regent Street stores with the aim of pushing exclusive and personalized marketing messages to shoppers via a common mobile phone app developed by the Crown Estate, which owns Regent Street.

Beacons and other wireless technologies are an easy and effective means for consumers to interact with physical retail experiences to get everything from coupons to content. Mobile shopping application ShopKick recently launched its shopBeacon platform that uses a shopper's in-store location to generate relevant promotions, rewards, and information related to the physical department around the user. Macy's successfully tried the technology and has rolled it out in its stores in San Francisco and New York. Shopkick has ambitious plans to embed the technology into thousands of retail stores over the next year. A slew of companies ranging from PayPal to Apple are all following suit, developing applications to help retailers enhance the physical shopping experience by giving customers everything from added-value content to simplified payment processes as well as making payment easier via mobile wallets and technologies, such as Apple Pay.

But it's still early days for beacons. "The ecosystem is just starting to take more shape," warns Preston Reed, founder of beacon and mobile technology company Footmarks. "We are only just seeing mobile publishers, audiences, physical spaces, infrastructure, and brands starting to come together."[17] Footmarks has already launched multiple beacon experiments for top brands, including sports teams, such as the Seattle Seahawks football team, which have installed beacons throughout their stadiums to give fans who have downloaded the team app special content and promotions on merchandise.

Despite such early success, Reed believes we are only just beginning to tap into the power of beacons. "The future of beacons is not just about promotions. It's going to be about customer service and engagement," says Reed. The Footmarks CEO refers to companies like AMC that are using mobile loyalty apps and beacons in their movie theaters to give customers exclusive film content. He evens sees new uses at grocery stores. "Imagine shoppers being able to leave virtual post-it notes on physical products, ensuring that your spouse never accidentally picks up the wrong product at the grocery store. Beacons will guide someone to the exact product your spouse wants you to pick up in order to cook tonight's recipe."

Even more interesting is Reed's speculation that some retailers may do nothing with beacons other than listen, particularly to better understand consumer behavior in their physical stores. In effect, beacons can become the physical equivalent of a brand listening program, silently tracking consumer sentiment and behavior in an anonymized but insightful way to help retailers adapt and improve their physical spaces.

Blurred Lines #2

As in product development, customer service, and advertising, a more synchronous and synergistic model is emerging between the digital and physical shopping experience. This phenomenon is often referred to as omnichannel retailing, which is in effect an increased blurring in the lines between online and off-line shopping. One of the more interesting aspects of this blurring is how companies are leveraging data from each side to inform and adapt the other.

For example, digital data and information can be used to adapt the physical shopping experience to better reflect the interests of customers. Target has been one of the leaders in using such techniques. Target has made extensive use of Pinterest to identify the most popular items in its store. Basically the most pinned Target items online are showcased not only at awesomeshop.target.com but also physically in Target stores, helping shoppers find the things that are resonating the most in the digital world. In effect, Target has recreated its Awesome Shop in a physical environment. Target has also capitalized on the first-party data supplied by Pinterest, not only to identify which items it should stock in its stores, but also to determine how many of a particular item it should stock at a given time, dependent on the number of pins an item receives.

Nordstrom, an upscale department store in the United States, is also using online insights provided by Pinterest to shape its in-store shopping experience. As at Target, in an attempt to highlight the online popularity of certain products, the most pinned Nordstrom products are physically tagged with a Pinterest logo in the store. Nordstrom is using adaptive tactics to tap into its customers' needs to simplify the shopping experience by curating the most popular items as determined by real-time Pinterest data.

Pinterest is not only changing the way stores present products, it is also determining the products they sell. Physical stores are becoming a real-time, real-life reflection of online destinations like Pinterest, a place that users have come to love and use to collect their favorite items.

For some retailers, the line is even blurrier. Yihaodian, an Asian online retailer of which Walmart owns 51 percent has decided to bypass brick-and-mortar stores altogether by opening up over 1,000 virtual stores across Greater China, essentially allowing consumers to shop via mobile phone by simply taking a photo of the QR code next to a product. Consumers still experience some sense of physical shopping, but they don't have to carry any heavy bags on the way home. All the goods are put into their online Yihaodian shopping basket and delivered to them at a later time and date. The Yihaodian virtual stores consist of posters and billboards located in places where consumers tend to have some downtime, such as at bus stops, public squares, and in subway stations. Since the launch of its virtual store initiative, Yiahoadian has seen a 17 percent increase in sales.

British fashion retailer Topshop took a similar virtual commerce approach when it debuted in China. Guests at the store's Beijing launch event tried on outfits, but used their phones and QR codes to make purchases, effectively turning the event into a mobile commerce opportunity. There wasn't a single cash register at the event. Topshop continues to take an online commerce only approach, using events and their physical advertising footprint to enable people to buy with their mobile phones.

Such virtual shopping models may be a glimpse of what's to come. According to the Jeff Cole of the Center for the Digital Future (CDF), "a lot of retail is seriously overbuilt. In the future you'll see only a third of the physical retail space we have right now. Brick-and-mortar stores will continue to decline in the future."[18] Cole even thinks this trend will move beyond just retailers into other distribution networks. "I predict in four years in some parts of the world automotive dealers will get out of the sales business and focus on the service business. Consumers will start buying autos via Amazon, which will schedule a test drive from your house rather than forcing a dealership visit. Everything else, including the financing and the actual purchase will take place online." Cole cites the Hyundai Equus dealership network, or lack thereof, as a possible future model. "Hyundai didn't have a dealership network appropriate for luxury customers so they had to start from scratch. With the Equus, Hyundai comes to your house for the test drive, you buy the car at your house, even the maintenance and support happens at your house. The consumer never goes to the dealership as they don't need to." Burred lines indeed.

This chapter covered the emerging use of data and technology to adapt everything from the price of a product to the purchase experience, both online of off-line (see Figure 5.3). In fact, adaptive marketers are increasingly exploring the blurred lines between those two worlds via showrooming, mobile apps, and beacon technology. The real-time data that is being generated from both off-line and online is proving to be an invaluable tool to create better virtual and physical shopping experiences, and perhaps to reinvent the entire model altogether.

So far we have explored all the various ways adaptive marketers are using data to adapt their marketing. In our next chapter we will explore how you turn your company into an adaptive marketing organization, one that thrives on quickly actioning data and the insight that comes with it to get closer to your customers and beat your competition.

Top Tips for Using Data to Improve Retail

1. Leverage data to ethically adapt pricing. Assess what new and existing data is available to help you adapt the price of your product or services in real time. Make sure the approach you take is ethical and doesn't discriminate.
2. Take e-commerce seriously. Amazon, Alibaba, and other large online retailers are growing and have big ambitions to sell virtually everything. Ensure you are tapping into the latest adaptive technologies to give you a competitive edge in those environments.

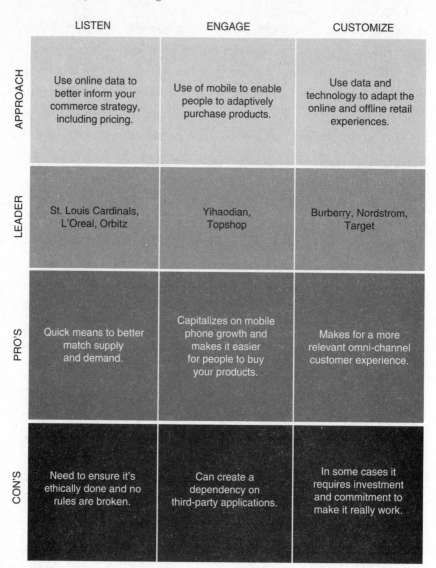

	LISTEN	ENGAGE	CUSTOMIZE
APPROACH	Use online data to better inform your commerce strategy, including pricing.	Use of mobile to enable people to adaptively purchase products.	Use data and technology to adapt the online and offline retail experiences.
LEADER	St. Louis Cardinals, L'Oreal, Orbitz	Yihaodian, Topshop	Burberry, Nordstrom, Target
PRO'S	Quick means to better match supply and demand.	Capitalizes on mobile phone growth and makes it easier for people to buy your products.	Makes for a more relevant omni-channel customer experience.
CON'S	Need to ensure it's ethically done and no rules are broken.	Can create a dependency on third-party applications.	In some cases it requires investment and commitment to make it really work.

Figure 5.3 Different Adaptive Approaches to Retail and Sales.

3. But don't forget physical sales. Even with the massive growth in e-commerce most people will still buy in physical locations, albeit via their mobile phone. Explore how mobile applications—yours or those of others—can help you beat the competition by delivering better value to your customers and more footfall into your shop.

4. Supercharge the retail experience. Experiment with new technologies such as beacons and RFID tags to adapt the physical retail experience in your favor.

5. Let online data inform off-line experiences—and vice versa. Explore digital proxy data, such as Pinterest pins, to adapt the physical experience or curate store items based on online trends.

CHAPTER 5.1

The Start-Up on Data

Vikesh Shah and Jim Downing

Metail

Given that clothing depends so heavily on the size of the individual, couldn't fashion retailers achieve better sales, lower returns, and happier customers if they understood the size and shape of customers?

Intuitively, it feels like the only logical answer should be yes. It is interesting to note then that in a world of increasing data and deeper understanding of customers, knowledge of the size and shape of shoppers still lags far behind. The Internet has facilitated a greater understanding of which items customers are interested in, their propensity to buy, causes of abandonment, and contact details. However, the industry has remained in quite a stagnant state when it comes to the size demographics of customers. Why is this the case?

Well, fundamentally, obtaining this information is difficult. Think about the length of time required for a tailor to take your measurements for a bespoke suit. Now multiply this by the millions of customers retailers have. In the absence of millions of tailors and effort required, the industry is dependent upon individuals measuring themselves and then choosing to share this information with retailers. This dependency means that the industry must provide something of value back to customers in order to incentivize customers to measure and share their size information.

Our approach hinges on the fact that when browsing online, customers cannot do the very thing that clothes are designed for—wear them. Customers cannot try on the clothes because they are not physically available. But what if body shape and garment fit visualization technologies could be harnessed to let customers see how clothes would look on their own body? Could that provide shoppers with enough incentive to share their size and shape data?

We tested this hypothesis during London Fashion Week SS15 with British designer Henry Holland. For the first time ever, during the live show, our virtual fitting room allowed online viewers of the show to see how the clothes worn by models would look on their own bodies—that is, they could virtually "try on" the clothes. In total, 76 percent of visitors to the site shared their size data to create their virtual models and spent 21 minutes on average trying on Henry's clothes. Such a high adoption rate and engagement shows that customers are willing to share their size data when asked in the correct way and provided with value back.

The benefit of size and shape data will initially come through providing a more personalized experience for fashion customers. Today, the current benchmark for personalized experience comes from personal shoppers. In addition to an understanding of trends, colors, and preferences, one of the skills of a personal shopper is knowledge of what styles work best for a customer's body shape. Once a customer's body shape is known, that same level of adaptive service can be delivered online. Take, for example, a lady who does not have a well-defined waist and would find that a shift dress flatters her figure. Instead of sending generic e-mail campaigns, why not send her a bespoke e-mail containing a personalized selection of shift dresses to help her find the right style of clothes for her figure. The idea can be expanded further into personalized editorial content whereby customers are shown different styling articles based depending upon their body shape.

Size data also has scope to improve the relevancy of online advertising. Retargeting has been a major success story in recent times. However, it can often lead to an infuriating customer journey when visitors return to an online shop, only to find the garment they were looking at is out of stock in their size. Linking together retargeting, stock and size data will help to prevent this frustrating experience and ultimately increase the likelihood of a retargeting sale for retailers.

Prospecting digital advertisements can also become a portal for collecting size data. The high adoption and engagement rate of Fitting Room means that we can help improve the click-through rates of prospecting ad units like these. Furthermore, once customers reach the fashion website, the retailer will already be armed with data on the customer's shape and therefore can provide a more personalized experience from the beginning, including reordering items listed on category pages according to what will fit customers best or simply hiding garments that are out of stock.

These approaches could be used not only to optimize conversions, but also to optimize sell-through of stock before marking it down. By bringing clothes that fit and suit the customers to their attention during sales, it could be possible to reduce the depth of price cuts—a bespoke selection of sales clothes that flatter the customer's shape. Cost of returns on marked-down goods is particularly high. Guiding price-sensitive customers to clothes that will fit and suit them might make it possible to either offer returns where they weren't previously offered or reduce return rates where they are.

We believe that digital technology and the specific size data we can collect on customers can dramatically help fashion marketers create better, more adaptive customer experiences. The technology is there, it's just time for retailers to try it on.

CHAPTER 6

Heavy Lifting

N ow you know the power of big data in all of its glorious shapes and sizes: small, secure, smart, synchronous, and, hopefully, secure. The question now is how to best prepare your organization to capitalize on that data: to get, manage, and action it faster than your competition. This chapter is called "Heavy Lifting" for a reason. Putting together your technology and data infrastructure is a key element to laying down the foundations for your future adaptive marketing ambitions. Without this there is a risk that you will simply drown in the coming data tsunami. With a solid infrastructure, you can move faster than ever before. Without one, you'll always be one step behind your customers and your competition. At least one step.

From Geneva with Love

Somewhere up in the Swiss Alps resides a sophisticated and futuristic mission control center full of high-resolution screens showing real-time reports from around the world. A dozen or so enthusiastic international youth are scattered around the room, often sharing intelligence with each other as they decipher the data streaming in on each of the large monitors. Periodically they jump out of their seats to stroll over and personally report the news back to their boss, who ingests all of this information and analyzes it at lightning speed. You could be forgiven for thinking you've stumbled into Ernst Stavro Blofeld's SPECTRE headquarters, but the boss is not bald and he's not stroking a white cat. Instead, the boss is Pete Blackshaw, Global Head of Digital Marketing and Social Media at worldwide food giant Nestlé, and the facility is the company's DAT room perched on to top of its headquarters overlooking beautiful Lake Geneva.

Blackshaw joined the company in 2011 with a mission to make it the most digitally savvy marketing organization in the packaged goods industry. No small task given that Nestlé has over 200,000 employees around the world, sells 1.2 billion products, and produces 1,500 pieces of original content each day. His task was to turn this conservative and traditional Swiss company into a fast, agile organization with digital at the very core of its approach to building brands and delighting consumers. Guided by Nestlé's "better, faster, smarter" mantra, Blackshaw started an ambitious journey to turn Nestlé's marketing people into not only good adaptive marketers but the best people in the business.

One of the first steps Blackshaw took was to launch his Digital Acceleration Team initiative, better known as the aforementioned DAT. The idea for the DAT emerged from one of Nestlé's first trips to Silicon Valley where Blackshaw and the senior management team spent time with dozens of start-ups and more established companies, such as Google and Facebook. "It was such an inspiring trip that we wanted to take a slice of it back to our HQ and work out how to rapidly scale the experience and more importantly the mentality across our organization," says Blackshaw. "The opportunity was to bottle up that same sense of speed and agility that you get with start-ups and share and embed it across Nestlé."

The DAT program is made up of a dozen managers from around the world who are rotated every eight months. Once they complete their rotation, these managers are sent back to their markets as newly trained adaptive marketers who can inspire and train others back in their home country. Like Jedi warriors, they are spreading the adaptive force person by person in each and every market.

During their time in Switzerland, DAT team members are exposed to the new trends of real-time marketing, getting involved in everything from managing social communities for global brands, monitoring and analyzing social listening data, to creating thought leadership, often via a live recording studio that regularly produces short video clips that are then dispersed throughout the organization. The DAT teams also undertake special projects, often based on requests from senior management. These projects have included everything from how to improve digital recipe solutions to "reverse mentoring" of top executives, who often drop by to demonstrate their strong support for the program via company-wide interviews in the DAT studio.

Since its inception, over 60 Nestle employees have gone through DAT training, and other markets have decided to create smaller versions of the program, including India, China, Italy, and Spain, and over a dozen more are planned.

Drilling for Oil

Nestlé's DAT room has multiple different streams of data coming in from a variety of sources, everything from Radian6 listening information to SocialBakers social statistics to Google trends. This data is what lights up the screens around the room, everything from TVs, to desktop computers, to tablets and mobile phones. Blackshaw's DAT team members are constantly monitoring all of this information, flitting between screens and data sets, analyzing and actioning the data to disparate parts of the business. The data is the key ingredient to making the DAT function on a daily basis. Data is in effect like oil; it's an essential element to keep your adaptive marketing engine running.

Finding this oil is arguably the first step to becoming an adaptive marketer. In short, you need to get your hands on some actual data, preferably the real-time variety. Unfortunately for many marketers, this can be the first stumbling block. Many organizations struggle to source data, even their own data, which can be highly fragmented and spread across the company in disconnected silos. Sometimes this fragmentation is intentional; many companies have data hoarders who purposefully limit access to their information in an attempt to gain leverage in the organization, effectively playing the old "knowledge is power" strategy for career success. In other cases, data hoarding is unintentional, with divisions or individuals simply not realizing how their information could be applied elsewhere. According to recent CompTIA research, 78 percent of US business and IT executives agreed that if they could actually harness all of their data, they'd have a much stronger business.[1]

In a first step to solving this problem, many marketers will embark upon a data discovery project, which is essentially an audit across their organization and the broader industry to identify existing or new data sources that have potential application on their own or by blending them with other information. Large data brokers and consultancies ranging from Acxiom to WPP to SAP provide such services. Nathan Summers, Global Chief Digital Officer at Jaguar Land Rover (JLR), worked with SAP to undertake such an initiative for the sprawling auto giant. "One of the first steps I took when joining was to identify and bring together all of our customer data into one place. It used to sit in different parts of the business and in different markets. We now have one single global data model."[2]

Businesses such as JLR will typically have four types of potential data sets that need to be tracked down or sourced and, ideally, centralized (see Figure 6.1).

The first type of data is a company's own endogenous data, which can include information stored in a myriad of databases including customer relationship management (CRM), sales, research, media results, website behavior, cookie data, and so on. This was JLR's primary focus

ENDOGENOUS	SOURCED	COMPLEMENTARY	EXOGENOUS
THE COMPANY'S OWN DATA, OFTEN IN SILOS	EXTERNAL DATA SOURCED FROM API'S	2ND AND 3RD PARTY DATA WITH POTENTIAL TO ENHANCE YOUR DATA	OUTSIDE DATA THAT CAN IMPACT THE BUSINESS
SALES	TWITTER	KANTAR	WEATHER
CRM	FACEBOOK	ACXIOM	NEWS
WEB	GOOGLE	DATALOGIX	CULTURE
SERVICES	RADIAN6	EXPERIAN	EVENTS

Figure 6.1 Find the Data.

with SAP, and it wasn't an easy one given the automotive model, which includes numerous stakeholders, everyone from dealerships to financing partners, and even roadside assistance.

"It took us two years to build the data model, but we now have complete visibility on our customers and can connect different parts of the business that we couldn't before." Summers provides a simple customer scenario that is now feasible with the centralized database. "Our customers travel, so it's important for us to know how to help them when they are in another country and need roadside assistance. With a global database the organization is able to synchronize data and adapt in real time across geographies."

The second bucket of data is sourced data not directly owned by JLR but highly relevant to its business. This category would include things like Facebook, Twitter, and Google data, typically piped into an organization via what is generally referred to in the industry as an API, the first of many bewildering acronyms that the marketing and technology industry seem to conjure up on a regular basis. API stands for application programming interface, which is essentially a data pipeline between companies, enabling information to travel from one location to another in a standardized and secure format. Most major companies offer an API under certain legal conditions. For example, Google, Twitter, Amazon, and many others provide data streams that can be directly imported into your company's IT systems, and then can be used to make real-time decisions and take real-time actions.

For example, Amazon has an API that sends its product and pricing information to other companies, who can in turn include that data on their websites so people can get the information or simply buy direct without having to go to Amazon. Credit card payments on websites are also often transacted via an API. The point is that APIs enable companies to make the Internet function for consumers by invisibly exchanging data and information in the background without the user's knowledge. APIs also can give you a lot of actionable insight into those customers.

The third source of data is complimentary data sets that can be pooled with a brand's endogenous data to enhance it. Companies like Kantar, Acxiom, Oracle's Datalogix, and Experian all offer this type of data, which is frequently used by marketers to enhance consumer insight, media targeting, and, increasingly, measurement. Kantar's Worldpanel aggregates millions of real purchases tracked over weeks, months, and years. The panel includes both off-line and online shopping data, which is a veritable treasure trove of information for marketers seeking to understand exactly what elements of their advertising are actually delivering sales. While brands don't own the data, and the information is carefully managed to protect consumer identity, this complimentary data does enable adaptive marketers to supercharge their existing data sets.

The fourth and final category is exogenous data, which may at a superficial level not seem directly relevant to the brand but could have a deep impact if used wisely. This category includes many of those small, singular sources of data that brands capture to adapt everything from media placement to pricing strategies. Weather is one recurring example. Fortunately the Weather Channel has made its comprehensive weather API widely available to developers and marketers. Unilever is using this weather API to adapt its advertising and to up-weight media spend on Vaseline in locations where there are stronger winds because the company knows product demand will be higher in those locations. Walmart has also partnered with the Weather Channel to develop statistical models that correlate weather activity with store sales at a zip code level. For example, Walmart now knows that when the weather is cloudy, windy, and warm people prefer to buy steaks. In contrast, when it's hot and dry with light winds, people go for hamburgers. Such nuances may seem minor, but according to Walmart when the company promotes hamburgers rather than steaks based on weather conditions, the result is an 18 percent improvement in hamburger sales. Walmart has codified thousands of other such correlations that it now uses to determine what products to promote under different weather conditions.

Top Tips on Finding the Data

1. Make sure finding data is a priority. The organization must be aligned around the need to surface disparate data and centralize

it for the greater good of the company and its customers. The benefits and the business case must be clear to everyone.

2. Build in a realistic time frame. It took JLR nearly two years to develop its centralized SAP customer database. Ensure the organization understands the commitment required to make such a database happen.

3. Find a professional partner. Think twice before doing this on your end. There are many companies specializing in data management that know how to navigate complex and conservative organizations to get things done.

4. Tap into APIs and complimentary data sets. APIs are often easily accessible and available, and big complimentary data sets can enrich your existing data.

5. Search for the silver bullets. Like Walmart, you should search for those special pieces of data, often small and singular, that can make a real impact on your business. Start with the weather.

Storing the Oil

Once you've got all the data, where do you put it? Well, if data is the oil, then you need to get yourself an oil depot, a place to securely keep and maintain all of this precious information that you have and will continue to collect (see Figure 6.2).

This seems straightforward, but once again many companies stumble at this stage. According to a recent study by the Chief Marketing Officer (CMO) Council and SAP, most marketers don't have the confidence that they have the tools or the people to manage

DATABASES   DMP   DATA FEEDS

Figure 6.2 Manage the Data.

their data. It's not that these companies don't have an existing database. It's more that they have dozens of databases, which are not always connected together, frequently contain dirty or uncleaned data, and cannot be turned into actions. According to that same CMO Council and SAP report, only 10 percent of marketing executives were highly confident in their company's ability to turn data into actionable intelligence.[3]

As a consequence many companies are turning to data management platform solutions, better known as a DMP. DMPs have proliferated like bunnies over the past few years in response to a growing need from the marketing community to have technology that can import and manage new and old data and make it actionable. Clunky old databases, reports, and spreadsheets of marketing results are all being swept aside in favor of these sophisticated data warehouses, which are built to store really any type of data, but particularly the real-time digital kind, such as APIs. Research by the Interactive Advertising Bureau (IAB) and Winterberry Group found that most marketers not only understand the need for a DMP but are well along the journey to implementing one.[4] For example, 92 percent of marketers said their company's interest in a DMP had increased over the past year, while 62 percent had already implemented one or planned to do so within the next year. Most of these marketers, up to 87 percent according to the IAB and Winterberry Group, typically use a DMP simply to improve their advertising ROI.

Sometimes DMP solutions store data on the Internet, in what is generally called a cloud-based solution, effectively eliminating the need for marketers to worry about the hassles of hosting or their IT departments. As with any other cloud solution, the data can be accessed anytime, anywhere, as long as there is Internet access. Cloud-based approaches make it easier for a brand's marketing partners, such as agencies, to input as well as access a harmonized and singular data set, ensuring everyone is acting on the same information in a coordinated way. In Nathan Summers' world, such a central database ensures that JLR's marketing, PR, and sales teams are looking at the same data, albeit with slightly different lenses and permissions.

When selecting a DMP solution, you should make sure that it nurtures and takes care of your data in at least four ways. First, the solution should normalize and standardize the data to make sure it's ingested correctly; in the process, bad data should be eliminated and the remaining data should fit into a common taxonomy so you know that it is correct and exactly what it represents. Second, a DMP should also enable marketers to deduplicate information that may have been accidentally or inadvertently entered twice into the system. Third, a good DMP should provide ample security to protect against hacking, data theft, and ensure industry or government data protection standards are being enforced. Fourth and finally, your DMP solution should be "open" enough to work with the broader technology ecosystem, which will help you action the data in a myriad of different ways.

It's important to highlight that government regulation on data protection is a critical issue when it comes to a DMP, particularly in the United States and European Union where politicians continue to pass legislation and directives while industry bodies push for more self-regulation. Any DMP solution needs to factor in these rules. In simplistic terms, consumers need to know what data is being stored on them. Furthermore, consumers need to grant data collection permission via easily accessible ways to opt in and opt out. JLR's Nathan Summers put customer permission first when developing his centralized data. "At every JLR customer touchpoint there is specific language to get customer permission," says Summers. "We use these permissions to govern how we use that data so we don't violate the trust and data contract that we've formed with people. In fact, at any given time our customers can update the permissions they've granted to us via our website."

Summers' efforts to protect JLR's consumer data is a reminder that what matters is not the efficiency of storing data via DMPs, but making sure that the company has clear principles and corresponding practices in the way it manages that information. Remember, successful adaptive marketers always put the customer first.

Top Tips on Managing the Data

1. Explore a DMP solution. Many market-leading solutions exist that can help you quickly manage disparate old and new data sources and apply that data to adaptive marketing solutions.
2. Ensure you remain "open." Whatever solution you select, ensure that it is an "open" one capable of working with other technologies that can help you action the data.
3. Expect changes. The DMP business is a relatively new industry, which is ripe for further consolidation. Revisit your solutions on a regular basis and make sure contractually that you have the right and means to take your data elsewhere if needed.
4. Use your DMP to align your marketing ecosystem. Make sure all of your internal marketing divisions, agencies, and other partners are contributing to and leveraging the same data and governance.
5. Put the consumer first. Make sure you've built in principles and practices into your data management approach that abide by all necessary regulation and best practice when it comes to putting consumers' trust first.

Refining the Oil

Back in Nestlé's DAT room, all of this sourced and stored data is swirling around in various shapes, sizes, and colors across all of Pete Blackshaw's screens. Small dots appear like a Georges Seurat painting across a Radian6 virtual map of the world, growing in size as certain trends begin to emerge or diminishing as the buzz on certain tracked topics dissipates. The visualizations are interpreting and making sense of all the raw data that has been sourced and stored by Nestlé; the process is essentially like refining the crude oil that has been put into the oil depot.

Data visualization and reporting have become key parts of the adaptive marketing engine and correspondingly another multimillion dollar industry. Marketers are desperate to find ways to intelligently view all this data they've been collecting and to bring some order to the chaos and confusion that can accompany the tsunami of data that can be collected (see Figure 6.3). According to a survey by Intel, 33 percent of companies surveyed are working with very large amounts of data (500 TB or more), and 84 percent of their IT managers are essentially working with unstructured data. Of seven possibilities put in front of them by Intel, these IT managers indicated that they would find the most value in receiving help deploying cost-effective data visualization methods, which is particularly important given that 63 percent of them expect all analytics to be done in real time in the future. Without any structure and intuitive visualization of the data, it's almost impossible to make fast adaptive marketing decisions.[5]

As marketing commentator Michael Palmer once blogged: "Data is just like crude. It's valuable, but if unrefined, it cannot really be

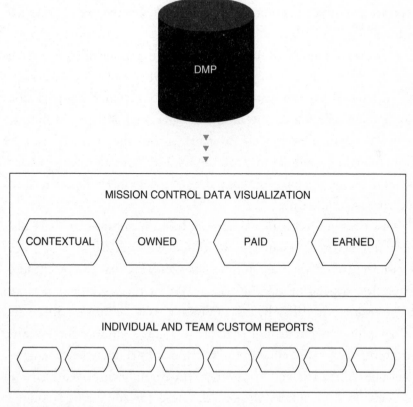

Figure 6.3 Report the Data.

used. It has to be changed into gas, plastic, chemicals, etc., to create a valuable entity that drives profitable activity; so must data be broken down, analyzed for it to have value."[6] Kimberly-Clark's Chris Whalen backs this up: "Fast-moving data can be meaningless. We are looking for structured, real or near-time data that is predictive and proxy data for our leading metrics rather than just random streams of information."

In short, by structuring and breaking down real-time data, companies are beginning to develop much better attribution reporting models that can determine exactly what is happening with their marketing investment. Google is one of those companies using reporting tools and visualization to help brands make more informed decisions. Google's Eileen Naughton adds, "We now have tools that use Android OS geolocation data to understand the correlation between a consumer search or a display advertisement and an actual in-store visit. There's a reporting and accountability of marketing dollars that we've never had before."

However, GroupM's Rob Norman warns that some of these attribution models may be too myopic and miss the bigger picture. "There is a big difference between countability and accountability. Many attribution models promote short-term use of data. A lot of the real-time data that flows into these models mitigates against long-term investment and vision. For example, an attribution model that only goes to 30 days is not the same as a long-term brand builder's attribution model, which is a customer's life time."

This attribution debate will rage on. In the meantime, you have dozens if not hundreds of data visualization tools to select from today, with a vast array of off-the-shelf and bespoke software that can be cheap or expensive, depending on your needs. All of these solutions perform a wide variety of different tasks. Visual.ly is a combined gallery and infographic generation tool that offers a simple toolset for building stunning data representations. "Computational knowledge engine" Wolfram Alpha lets you create nice, intelligently displayed charts in response to data queries without the need for any configuration. It leverages a lot of publically available data, and therefore it doesn't even require a connection to your own data in many cases. IBM's Many Eyes allows you to quickly build visualizations from publically available or uploaded data sets and features a wide range of analysis types, including the ability to scan text for keyword density and saturation. Gephi is a graph-based visualizer that takes large data sets and produces beautiful visualizations, including identifying social nodes related to each other. For example, you could use the tool to visualize and identify that Ellen DeGeneres followers on Twitter are also big followers of the International House of Pancakes.

Where and how does all of this visualization take place? Like Nestlé, many companies have established mission control centers or war rooms, where cross-functional teams gather to analyze the data. Unilever, Pepsi, JLR, Mondelez are just a few of the companies that have developed or used such NASA-like rooms to interpret real-time data and make real-time decisions on how to adapt their marketing activities. The only constraints on what you want to visualize in these rooms is the data itself and, of course, what's important for the people in the room to analyze. Most big marketing teams will visualize four key data categories in their mission control centers.

Mission Control Data Visualization Categories

1. Contextual media: the broader cultural context in which a brand's consumers and target audience are living, including the news and overall trending topics.
2. Owned media: all of the brand's owned data, most of it from the endogenous sources referenced in the first section, including the brand's website data, sales information, Facebook brand page performance, etc.
3. Paid media: data on the brand's paid media performance, including performance data on off-line and online advertising.
4. Earned media: the social listening data, PR, and other forms of word-of-mouth advertising that give the brand insight into issues and possible opportunities as well as measuring the impact of marketing.

Mission control rooms are often used during big events, such as the Superbowl and the Oscars, which as demonstrated in previous chapters, provide large-scale opportunities for brands to have a voice and relevance with their target audience. However, the challenge for most brands is to use these mission control rooms on a regular basis, perhaps weekly, maybe even daily at times when the foundational and adaptive layers are in full swing, such as product launches. These ongoing adaptive mission control meetings don't require a cast of thousands, just an ongoing core cross-functional team of people who can analyze the information and act on it.

JLR's Nathan Summers is taking just such an approach with a firmer governance model that complements that company's ambitious data centralization initiative. "We are going to enforce cooperation through governance. People need to understand if something happens in one part of the organization, it can impact someone else's job. People need to start talking to each other more frequently and start thinking about the implications that their data may have across other functions."

In addition to larger cross-functional mission control room meetings, JLR is also dispersing its visualized data across disparate parts of the business, almost like tiny little mission control rooms on people's desktop computer, tablet, or even smartphone. Each of these individual reports can be customized for particular audiences to drive up relevance but also to ensure that confidential information, particularly consumer data, is properly managed and distributed only to those with authorization. Eventually, every JLR employee will have access to relevant real-time data so he or she can make daily adaptive marketing decisions.

Top Tips on Data Visualization and Reporting

1. Pick a reporting and visualization tool. Many DMPs will provide some level of reporting, but explore your options to see if there are more intuitive and useful visualization tools on the market.
2. Set up your mission control room(s). Establish a physical data visualization hub and use that room to bring together cross-functional teams to make adaptive decisions across the organization.

3. Establish a governance model. Ensure that people are working together and understand the implications of their data for other parts of the business.
4. Arm your employees with the relevant data. Develop mini mission controls so your employees can also tap into the data and act on it in their daily job.
5. Develop a reporting architecture. Determine who in the organization will get access to what levels of data and how. Ensure that you protect customer and confidential data.

Using the Oil

At long last we have come to the final bit of heavy lifting. You've now built your adaptive marketing engine: you've sourced the data, centralized and secured it into a DMP, and put in the tools and created the physical space to structure and visualize all the information. Now it is time to do something with that data, to put that oil into action, which will happen in two primary ways (see Figure 6.4).

The first way to action the data is by using algorithms and technology, literally codifying the learning identified over time that your organization should operationalize throughout the business: Walmart's understanding that certain weather conditions lead to more hamburger purchases, Orbitz's realization that your operating system impacts your propensity to spend on a hotel, Netflix's identification of new programs and content through viewing patterns. These repeated statistically significant correlations and causations are too often *not* captured by companies and shared across the organization. Instead, companies keep relearning the same old things or, even worse, forgetting about them. Good adaptive marketers develop repeatable algorithms—that is, effectively code—either on their own or in partnerships with other companies. In fact, some marketers such as Unilever are even sponsoring "hackathons." These events bring together internal teams, sometimes even with start-ups or outside talent, to collaborate and create new applications that are either consumer-facing or internally focused ways of automating intelligence and acting on it.

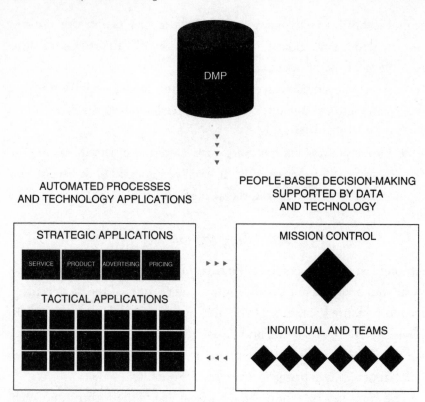

Figure 6.4 Action the Data.

Some of these applications can be simple tactical tools. Other applications are bigger and bolder technology platforms that represent companies' much larger ambitions to embed adaptive marketing techniques throughout their business. Programmatic marketing, which we covered in chapter 4, is a great example of this secondary, more strategic category. Brands, such as Unilever, Nestlé, P&G, Ford, Kimberly-Clark, and American Express, are investing heavily in developing a programmatic solution for their business that codifies and scales their approach to adaptive media and creative.

If the first means to action data is via algorithms and technology, the second path to action is via analysis and talent. Yes, the good old-fashioned method of people sitting in their mission control rooms or interpreting the data in a visualized report on their tablet. The challenge for adaptive marketers is to help these people analyze and action data and insight correctly and fast, much faster than the laborious process most companies have used in the past. Making decisions quickly requires companies to develop rules, the decision-making guidelines that will help equip people when the moment arrives. As JLR's Summers states: "Adaptive is not an excuse to be a cowboy. You still need to have rigour to prioritize and to make sure everything ladders up to the broader brand and its ambitions."

In other words, to be adaptive requires some advance preparation that will save time, energy, and possibly mistakes later on. In fact, this preparation may make up the vast majority of time required to be adaptive; the actual act of adaptive marketing may be minor in comparison to the hours required to prepare for the various scenarios that may or may not happen.

Top Tips on People-Based Adaptive Decisions

1. Get totally aligned on the brand. Marketing teams need to completely agree on the brand and its voice, including everything from the brand's character, visual identity, personality, and appropriate media channels. Hold a workshop and get all of your internal and external brand stakeholders, including legal, on the same page. Literally write it down.
2. Identify your broader brand territory. What is the brand's broader contextual territory? How does that define your listening strategy? What events—big or small, your own or those of others—could produce issues or opportunities for the brand?
3. Develop a list of possible triggers. What actions would occur around these events or spontaneously that would require or could lead to a response from the brand? When that trigger occurs, who is best placed in the organization to respond? What are the rules around responses, including timing and approvals?
4. Ensure that triggers can be prioritized. Not every trigger is equal. Make sure to categorize triggers and immediately action those with a high level of severity or importance.
5. Budget for adaptive responses. Ensure you have an adaptive budget in case it's required in order to properly respond to a situation.

All of these elements combine to help teams understand what is appropriate or inappropriate for the brand in certain situations and how best to respond to these scenarios. For example, Unilever's Axe deodorant marketing team had done its homework on the brand's values on same-sex marriage during a stakeholder alignment session. That homework paid off when it gave the Axe marketing team the confidence to tweet a supportive message during a performance by singer Macklemore at the Grammy Awards during which thirty couples, including some same-sex couples, were married on stage. Axe took advantage of another trigger in its broader brand territory by quickly tweeting and posting an apology to the United Kingdom's Prince Harry when he was photographed nude with some girls in Las Vegas; the implication here was that Axe deodorant was too successful in attracting girls and leading him astray.

Los Obstaculos

As always there will be obstacles on the way to becoming an adaptive marketer. Fortunately, you can at least be aware of them by learning from the mistakes made by others and adopting and adapting the solutions they have put in place.

One of the biggest issues many adaptive marketers face is their company's very unadaptive and inflexible budgeting process. Most companies are not readily set up to fund things at a moment's notice, which means any desire to respond in real time typically gets bogged down in chasing the necessary funds from preallocated budgets. To solve this issue, companies like Kimberly-Clark have established a fluid adaptive budget specifically to be used for the real-time scenarios that may come up in a mission control room. As a general guideline it is recommended that brands set aside roughly 10–20 percent of their existing digital budgets to create an "always on" adaptive pot of money that can be used as events are triggered.

Coca-Cola has long been a champion of this type of codified approach to financing broader innovation. The global beverages giant has developed its 70/20/10 model for financing marketing investments. In the Coca-Cola model 70 percent of the budget should go to proven low-risk investments and activities. The next 20 percent of the budget should go to activities that have been tested and have demonstrated some success, enough to warrant additional investment. The final 10 percent of investment should be allocated to new activities where the organization has little knowledge or experience and therefore faces greater risk. This last 10 percent isn't cash thrown away to any whimsical idea. A rigorous due diligence process is in place to assess all innovation opportunities. In the end, what the 70/20/10 model does is encourage Coca-Cola's marketers to take some risk, experiment with new technologies and innovations, and keep on adapting.

The second major obstacle for many adaptive marketers is content. Even with all the data and technology and talent in the world, without any actual content to action there is very little you can do in many situations. In short, there is nothing to feed the adaptive beast. As GroupM's Rob Norman states "What adaptive marketing demands is a bigger number of creative assets and more flexible assets."

Smart adaptive marketers like Kimberly-Clark are developing creative assets in advance and storing this content in asset libraries. Marketers can then tap into this asset bank when needed to quickly deploy content in adaptive situations, thus saving production time and costs. These assets are typically standardized and include preapproved templates and images that can be repurposed and reassembled with a light layer of new creative. WPP's Hogarth is one company that specializes in this sort of approach to content development and storage.

Other asset development requires more sophisticated approaches and can be sourced or created in a variety of ways. Some marketers and agencies have established adaptive content studios, particularly when it comes to short video clips. WPP's Possible specializes in rapid video clip development, most recently producing hundreds of short films for mobile phone brand HTC to use as and when needed as part of its #creatography campaign.

Other marketers are partnering with publishers to source assets. Unilever recently formed a partnership with the United Kingdom's

Guardian newspaper to tap into its Guardian Labs team of journalists to create ongoing microcontent for its various brand social newsfeeds, particularly regarding its corporate responsibility initiatives for sustainability. Auto brand MINI has successfully partnered with hip online news company Buzzfeed to cocreate a series of custom social posts centered around the marketing slogan "Not Normal," The content drew over one million engagements and successfully provided the adaptive content MINI so urgently required. Virgin Mobile took things a step further with BuzzFeed and launched a first-of-its-kind 24/7 newsroom that created content and responded to social conversations in real time with interesting, timely, and brand-relevant content aligned with pop culture. In total over 190 pieces of original branded content were created, garnering nearly ten million views in total.

Companies such as NewsCred and Percolate also help feed the adaptive beast with content. Both companies aggregate published stories and content from the likes of *Forbes*, the *New York Times*, and the *Economist*. Brands can then pay for various packages that give them the right to adapt and republish that content in their own marketing ecosystems. For example, the content could be used within programmatic advertising units as well as with social newsfeeds. Brands as diverse as Kimberly-Clark and Dell have tapped into these companies to close the content gap and ensure their adaptive marketers are properly equipped when they most need it.

A robust adaptive marketing engine will go a long way toward making your company a more agile, responsive organization, closer to its customers, and faster than its competitors (see Figure 6.5). However, it's not the only element required. JLR's Nathan Summers hit upon arguably the biggest factor that makes adaptive marketing work when he said that JLR must be "more impatient." What he meant was the company's culture had to change. The day-to-day behavior and the overall mind-set of the people in the organization had to get used to moving faster, collaborating closer, not fearing data and technology, but loving these twin engines of potential insight and growth.

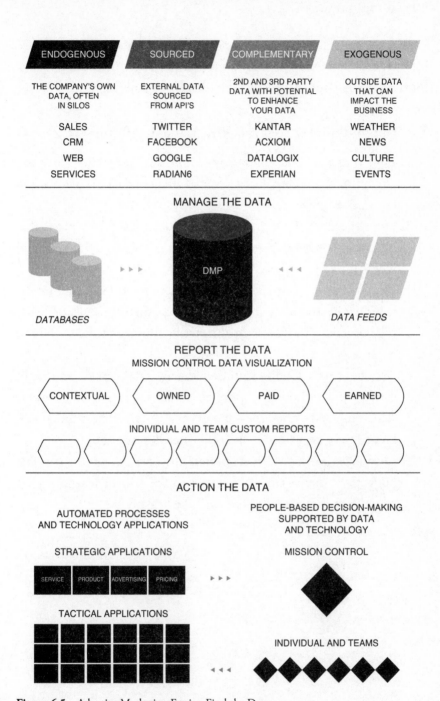

Figure 6.5 Adaptive Marketing Engine Find the Data.

We now move past the heavy lifting of data, technology, and process into the lighter touch that is the secret sauce that's truly need to transform a company into an adaptive marketing organization.

Top Tips for Building Your Adaptive Marketing Engine

1. Find your data. Audit your own company to identify what you already have, and tap into external sources of data to enhance and enrich that information.
2. Store the data. Ensure you have a robust DMP in place that ingests and harmonizes all of this data to make it actionable and secure.
3. Report the data. Use the latest visualization tools to structure the information so that people can find meaning in it. Establish a mission control to drive cross-functional usage of the visualized data.
4. Action the data. Codify your learning in strategic or tactical applications and technology. Develop a robust process that ensures that teams have done their homework and have clear guidelines and rules to be adaptive when they need or want to.
5. Eliminate or mitigate the common obstacles. Don't let inflexible budgets or the lack of content get in the way of reaching your adaptive ambitions. Feed the adaptive beast.

CHAPTER 6.1

The Enterprise Solution on Data

Jeffrey K. Rohrs

Vice President, Marketing Insights

Salesforce

In 2013, the pinnacle of adaptive marketing, at least in advertising, was a single image tweeted by Oreo during the infamous Super Bowl XLVII blackout. Captioned "You Can Still Dunk in the Dark," the tweet was opportunistic, creative, quick-witted, and it came to symbolize the power of brands living in the moment in order to capitalize on cultural memes. With one burst of creativity, Oreo generated more brand awareness and positive sentiment than any of the other advertisers paying millions for commercial time.

With that kind of ROI, it was no wonder that other brands rushed to capitalize on this agile and adaptive marketing thing, only to be burned by their ham-handed attempts at cultural humor. Indeed, today's marketing is replete with examples of brands that, in trying to hack the culture, actually created their own PR disasters. Most recently, after one brand posted all of its Super Bowl XLIX tweets *the day before the game*, noted social media expert Scott Monty suggested that it was time to reassess this agile approach to marketing.

As successful as it was, the Oreo tweet was a snowflake on the mountain of potential held by adaptive marketing. The future of adaptive marketing is in leveraging the forces of connectivity, mobility, social media, and big data to better serve the customers. It is about knowing who your customers are—online and off-line—in order to provide the most relevant information, products, and services to fuel their journey from prospect to customer to loyal advocate. Today, we can see adaptive marketing's nascent promise in three emerging areas: social advertising, predictive intelligence, and connected devices.

Social Advertising

Facebook, Twitter, SnapChat and other social media networks are home to the real-time conversations of millions of people around the world. As these networks look to monetize their user relationships, they have become proving grounds for adaptive marketing's promise. Instead of renting the attention of an anonymous audience to advertisers, social advertising gives brands the ability to target precise consumer segments based on real-time demographics, psychographics, and behavioral insights. Moreover, these networks increasingly give advertisers the ability to layer in their own knowledge of their customers in order to differentiate messaging and target look-alike audiences in order to attract new customers.

In practice, this means that advertisers can now target their email subscribers who are also fans on Facebook in order to reinforce a campaign message—a practice that one leading retailer found increased intent to purchase by 22 percent. Such real-time targeting is already becoming more granular, allowing social advertisers to serve different creative based on both online and off-line behaviors. From the perspective of social advertising, adaptive marketing becomes a means by which to increase advertising efficiency and response while building multichannel relationships with customers.

Predictive Analytics

Whereas social advertising leverages consumer insights to power engagement via third parties, predictive analytics seeks to improve customer engagement within your own ecosystem of websites, mobile apps, and stores. The goal is to generate a single, ever-evolving view of each of your customers that can be used to personalize content, offers, and experiences in order to boost response, ROI, and brand loyalty. This effort is not only happening in real time but also inherently adaptive—changing product recommendations based on each customer's own changing interests and behaviors over time.

Connected Devices

A world with more connected devices translates into a future with untold numbers of adaptive marketing opportunities. Take New England BioLabs (NEB), for instance. The manufacturer of enzymes and reagents for the life sciences industry has long provided customers with branded freezers in which to store their products. However, until recently, those freezers failed to give NEB or its customers any insights into what products were in stock. As a result, researcher customers were often frustrated to discover they were out of a needed enzyme only after checking the freezer.

Enter the smart freezer. NEB modified its freezers so that researchers can remove products only after they have logged into the unit and scanned the products they remove. That information—the who, what, and when of product usage—is then sent to NEB's Salesforce-powered cloud application, which then has perfect, real-time visibility into inventory at every customer location. This, in turn, allows the company to replenish inventory before the customer even knows that something is running out—true adaptive marketing in action.

As social advertising, predictive analytics, and connected devices evolve, we're certain to see even more instances of adaptive marketing in action. But behind each story, there will have to be marketers willing to think differently about their roles. Adaptive marketers do not only sell, they work to serve each customer throughout their journey, leveraging the power of mobile, social media, connectivity, and data to deliver personalized, real-time experiences that exceed expectations for all involved. Adaptive marketers also collaborate with the product, technology, and operational teams within their organizations to foster innovation that transcends the ordinary and puts the customer at the center of everything they do.

In short, adaptive marketing is about much, much more than timely tweets. It's about transforming your business into a true customer company.

CHAPTER 7

Light Touch

Your adaptive marketing engine will play a fundamental role in providing the company with the essential data and technology infrastructure to scale and support your ambitions. However, this foundation alone will not create a fast and dynamic organization. Other factors are just as critical, particularly the company's culture as well as the behavior and makeup of its talent. In this chapter we explore the "light touch" required from all kinds of people across the organization. Often, these softer skills are the essential ingredient to success or failure on the road to becoming an adaptive marketing organization. And often this light touch will need to start with you.

Leading from the Front

"All of it has been difficult," laughs Keith Weed, Chief Marketing and Communication Officer of multinational consumer goods company Unilever. Weed was responding to a question regarding the biggest obstacle he has faced in his journey to turn his marketing team into an agile, data-friendly organization. Since taking the top marketing role in 2000, Weed has worked tirelessly to push his talent into not just adopting digital marketing and data, but embracing them as fundamental to the company's future. "It's taken lots of blood, sweat, and tears," adds Weed.

From day one Weed had a vision for where he wanted to take the organization. However, the plan itself wasn't always so clear, mainly because things kept evolving. For example, Weed points outs that during his five-year tenure the gargantuan mobile-heavy Facebook of today bears little resemblance to the burgeoning PC-based social network that existed when he first started. In fact, it's this constant adaption in his plans that is remarkable. Weed not only has a vision for Unilever as adaptive marketers, he's willing to constantly adapt his own plans to get them there.

"There was no road map," concedes Weed. "Consultants call it emerging strategy, you and I would call it making it up as you go along." Weed preferred to move with speed, and to accept the fact that there would be mistakes along the way. "We've made bets where we've had to do a U-turn," says Weed, "but in the end we've made more good bets than bad bets. Sometimes we've been lucky, but as Napoleon once said I prefer lucky generals over clever ones."

Weed is of course showing some typical English humility. You don't fundamentally change the culture of such a massive organization with just luck. The reality is that Keith Weed has demonstrated arguably the most important element in transforming a company from a conservative, traditional, slow-moving organization into one that embraces the speed, innovation, and data of adaptive marketing. In short, Weed was demonstrating leadership, which may at first sound trite and predictable, but routinely surfaces as a persistent predictor of success during any such transformational initiative. In a recent McKinsey study, senior management support (or lack thereof) was the biggest factor in determining the success or failure of change programs.[1] Without clear leadership, things don't change; in fact, they usually get worse.

Weed's commitment to move fast, to not fear failure, and to lean heavily into all things digital and data has given his people the confidence and freedom to do the same. Without such leadership most organizations remain paralyzed, with layer after layer of management and talent frightened to stick their neck out for fear of failing or breaking the traditional accepted ways of doing things (see Figure 7.1). The fact that Weed himself has had such a long tenure reinforces confidence within the organization that whatever he is doing is not only working, it's fully supported by the Unilever board as well.

TOP 3 FACTORS

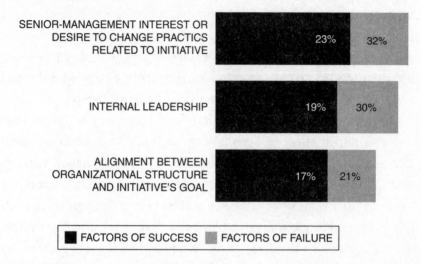

Figure 7.1   Factors That Contribute Most to Success, or the Absence of Which Contributes Most to Failure, of Companies' Past Digital Initiatives.

Source: Exhibit from "Bullish on Digital: Mckinsey Global Survey Results," August 2013, Mckinsey.

However, leadership also requires more than just words; it requires action, and Weed has taken plenty during his time in leadership. One of the first steps he took was to take a hard look at his talent to assess whether these employees were up to the challenge. According to Weed, there was a layer of Unilever management that made up a lost generation of digital marketing, which he roughly defines as those around 35–45 years old. "They are not old enough like me to have children in the house using digital, but also not young enough to be digital natives." The message Weed sent them was unequivocal; things had forever changed, and in his words: "If you are not prepared to make yourself capable in digital and data, nobody else is going to do it for you. You must commit or go find another career." Weed himself tweets nearly every day.

What Weed did offer this lost generation was intensive training, up to 8–10 days every year, including the well-known Hyper Island training program. Hyper Island has become something of a badge of honor for many in the marketing industry. The company offers a range of different corporate training sessions, including a three-day Digital

Acceleration Master Class designed to get people out of their comfort zone and into today's fast-paced world of technology and digital media. Large organizations will often send their lost generations to these intensive sessions, and after three days of challenging workshops, in-depth presentations, and hands-on activities, they emerge inspired, informed, and ready to boldly go where no marketer has gone before.

Unilever also established a Digital Academy, partly to ensure there was a sustained effort to keep its staff trained in the latest technologies, but also to keep its people and their behavior aligned with the new cultural norms Weed was espousing, in particular, the need to fail fast rather than slowly. Weed's passion comes through on the subject as he makes an analogy to athletes: "We need to value training the same way it's valued in sports. We need to keep using these new muscles or else they disappear again." This analogy to sports training is also mentioned by other senior marketing leaders at other organizations. For example, Chris Whalen at Kimberly-Clark frequently talks about exercising people's muscles and preparing them for the future. "Training, training, training," repeats Weed.

While Keith Weed and his counterparts are not going to work wearing a tracksuit and whistle, they are essentially playing the same critical role a coach does on a sports team. They are defining the overall playbook, constantly preparing their players—new and old—through exercise, providing the right equipment, and adapting the team and its tactics as the game unfolds. As Vince Lombardi, the legendary Green Bay Packers football coach, once said, "Leaders are made not born." The same applies to adaptive marketing leaders.

Top Tips for Leading Adaptive Change

1. Articulate the vision. Ensure that the company knows your adaptive vision, what that future looks like, and why it's fundamental to the company.
2. Build confidence and momentum. Repeat that vision over and over again, and instill the confidence into your management team and staff that they have your blessing to make change happen.

3. Don't fear failure. Not everything will go according to plan. Find the right balance of speed and innovation backed by good but fast decision making. Praise and encourage rapid success. Learn from fast but informed failure. Minimize slow and uninformed failure.
4. Train your staff. Equip your people to succeed; exercise those new muscles, and this applies particularly to the lost generation.
5. Change and adapt the plan. Practice what you preach. Assess the data and adapt your plan as time goes on and things change.

Revenge of the Nerds

The marketing industry is awash with stories on advertising's evolution from *Mad Men* to "Maths Men", that is, a shift from the right-brained, chain-smoking, heavy-drinking advertising talent of yesteryear to this new breed of left-brained, statistically minded, techno-nerds. The reality is not that binary; as mentioned earlier, the alchemy between both sides of the brain conjures up the best innovation and magic. Nonetheless, clearly something is changing.

Gartner bullishly predicted that within five years, by 2017, CMOs will be spending more on IT than CIOs (chief information officers).[2] In fact, when CMO Keith Weed talks about his transformation agenda at Unilever, technology is one of the first things to come up. "When I started in my role, our marketing technology was all over the place," says Weed. "One of the first steps I took was to make sure that we moved to one consistent global marketing technology platform."

This rising trend for CMOs to take a more active role in IT investment decisions has accelerated as digital marketing has increased in importance vis-à-vis more traditional marketing methods. In today's marketing world, CMOs have no choice but to get more involved in the IT infrastructure that increasingly plays a fundamental role in the day-to-day functioning of marketing, whether that means managing Facebook social marketing initiatives or running programmatic advertising campaigns. It's simply impossible to avoid technology anymore. According to an Accenture survey, over half of the CMOs surveyed rank marketing IT at or near the top of their priorities.[3]

In many cases this trend has caused friction between the worlds of the CMO and the CIO. According to Accenture's 2012 CMO-CIO Disconnect Study, only one in ten marketing and IT executives believes collaboration between CMOs and CIOs is at the right level in his or her organization (see Figure 7.2). [4] The study simply quantifies what many have suspected; the traditional lines between these two functions continue to blur.

Many companies are exploring ways to bridge this gulf. One way is through good old-fashioned process and governance. Consulting firms, such as Accenture, offer services that help to patch up the divide through workshops and methodologies. Other companies are looking at fresh talent to act as a personal bridge between CMO and CIO, someone capable of speaking the languages of both worlds and making sure the two are completely connected for the greater good.

Enter the Chief Data Officer and the Chief Digital Officer.

Either one of these CDO roles has become one of the hottest jobs in town, with a surge in hiring across industries as companies struggle with growing data and digital issues. According to IBM, 25 percent of Fortune 500 firms now employ a Chief Data Officer, who are typically responsible for establishing a much greater focus and optimized use of

NEED FOR COLLABORATION ACROSS THE C SUITE (%)

AMOUNT OF COLLABRATION

HIGH ● ● ● ● ● LOW

CMO					
WITH CIO	13	17	28	29	12
CIO					
WITH CMO	11	20	28	31	11

Figure 7.2 Marketing and IT Executives Citing the Need for More Collaboration between the CMO and CIO.

Source: Copyright © Accenture, CMOCIO Disconnect 2014.

data throughout the organization as well as for managing data risk.[5] "The Chief Data Officer makes sure that the information is accessible, managed, and governed in an orderly way, and it requires policy decisions and decisions about what information has value," says Debra Logan, an analyst at Gartner who studied this growing trend to hire CDOs. "Chief Information Officers typically can't tell you what kind of rights the company has around data, how it can be collected, how it can anonymized and what rules apply to the use of data."[6]

CDOs not only require specific skill sets, they also must have particular character traits in order to succeed. It's most often a role that requires an immense amount of soft power in order to influence an organization without the usual luxuries of direct reports and massive departments. In fact, according to research by Data Blueprint, only 45 percent of CDOs have a staff, and 48 percent of CDOs have no budget.[7] Perhaps this is why CDOs sometimes directly report to the CEO rather than to the CMO or the CIO; a mandate from the most senior person in the organization makes everyone take notice. The move also elevates the position from a bridge to an arbitrator, someone capable of rising above both worlds to get decisions made on behalf of everyone. According to Data Blueprint, nearly 80 percent of companies surveyed said a Chief Data Officer should report to the business side, not to IT. Regardless of the reporting lines, and there are many variations, there are some common and fundamental characteristics used when describing the CDO role.

Top 10 Traits of a CDO

1. Balance of technology and business skills
2. Highly influential with people and able to develop soft power
3. Strong leadership skills used to communicate a vision effectively
4. Ability to create cross-functional and collaborative teams
5. Entrepreneurial, self-starter

Of course it's more than C-level leadership that is required in organizations to realize adaptive marketing ambitions. With all the training in the world sometimes you still need to bring in new talent to help drive the cultural change and momentum so many companies desperately need. Often this is replacing the lost generation Keith Weed previously mentioned, the 35–45-year-olds who simply can't come to terms with all the change happening around them.

This lost generation is typically being replaced by a new generation of talent not only comfortable with data but also able to analyze it rapidly and act on it quickly. Tom Buday, Head of Marketing and Consumer Communication at Nestlé, succinctly captures this new talent requirement: "Using data to inform decisions and better serve customers has been around a long time. What's fundamentally changing is the speed and pervasiveness of data, and with that we must become better data collectors and analysts; more skilled at connecting dots."[8] According to a survey by *The Future Buzz*, 37 percent of companies surveyed said they are in desperate need of this type of new talent with serious data skills.[9]

There appear to be three types of data skill sets most in demand in the industry (pay close attention, parents with a child about to go to college).

Data scientists. These are the Jedi of the data world, individuals who not only know the nuts and bolts of data, but who can also deftly develop sophisticated new algorithms and applications of this information to help a company's broader business goals. The *Harvard Business Review* has described this role as the sexiest of the twenty-first century. Data scientists normally come up through the ranks from the analyst position. While finding them can be tough, thinking laterally across industries, even in academia, can surface fresh talent looking for bigger adventures elsewhere.

Data engineers. These are the people in the engine room doing much of the heavy lifting described in chapter 7. Without these engineers, you'd be looking at data that is badly managed, unstructured, and, even worse, unsecure. Typically with a technology background, these people can be sourced from universities through consultancies and the new cloud-based marketing solution firms such as Salesforce and Adobe.

Data analysts. The day-to-day analysts responsible for assessing data, finding insights and information from it, and deciding on what actions to take. Look for smart employees with a statistical background from universities around the world.

Top Tips for Finding Adaptive Talent

1. Clarify the roles of the CMO and the CIO. Make sure there is proper alignment and governance between these two leaders and their organizations, particularly as digital can lead to a greater obfuscation between the two realms.
2. Hire a CDO. If the organization requires someone to better connect the dots on all things digital and/or data, think about hiring someone who can to take the lead and help the company avoid obstacles, rise above the politics, and move faster.
3. Tap into the new generation. If you can't retrain the lost generation or simply need to inject new skill sets, hire new talent, particularly in the area of data, which appears to be the current pain point for so many companies.
4. Understand what data talent you need. Determine what skills sets are required before starting your search. Given the time is takes to find a good data scientist, engineer, or analyst, you need to know exactly what you are looking for at the outset.
5. Think laterally when looking for the talent. Data experts are hard to find and expensive. Look at other industries, even in academia, where data-friendly talent may be looking for a new challenge. Universities across the world may be home to talent looking for a move elsewhere.

The Circle of Life

Once you've hired all of these tech and data geeks, you may be wondering where to put them. In short, what's the best structure to put in place to move faster, break down silos, and truly become an adaptive marketing organization?

Unfortunately there is no easy straightforward answer as there are many different models being embraced by companies (see Figure 7.3). One size does not fit all. Different factors can influence a company's exact structure, including market nuances, legacy businesses, personalities, digital sophistication, budgets, and so on. Even politics can get in the way. Kimberly-Clark's Chris Whalen drily commented: "When you throw out the word 'adaptive' everyone wants to own the idea."

In fact, Whalen's organization took what is usually the first step in rolling out an adaptive marketing structure when it experimented with the new model in just a few markets with a few brands. There are various names for this approach, including lighthouse trials or beta tests. Whatever the term, the approach typically allows companies to stick their toes in the water and prove that all the talk around adaptive actually does deliver results as well as some precious learning. This approach also creates the much needed proof points and repeatable models that can then be embraced and exploited by the rest of the business. Such an approach is typically best suited for decentralized companies much like Kimberly-Clark. As Whalen says, "It would have been

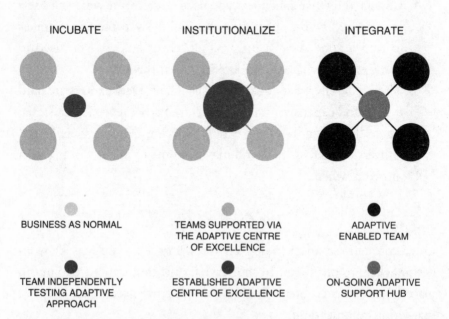

Figure 7.3   Three Adaptive Operational Structures.

easy to do an ivory-tower mandate. Instead, we developed several pilots that were executed in different ways. Some very structured processes, others more swarm-based and more informal. Out of these pilots we then developed best practice based on what actually worked."

For simplicity's sake we will call this an "incubation" approach as it essentially enables smaller-scale, shielded tests to quickly occur without the full weight of the organization slowing down the effort. There are, of course, some weakness to such an approach. It can slow down your efforts or at least the perceived efforts to impact the broader business, which can largely remain unaware of the small-scale test happening without widespread participation. Sometimes the full adaptive marketing engine may not yet be in place given its frequent dependencies on enterprise level solutions. Finally, there's a chance the incubated project may not succeed due to some unforeseen circumstances, and this may result in the new approach inadvertently failing due to some sort of anomaly. Nonetheless, many companies still opt for this incubation approach because it is it's a low-risk, quick-result means of proving the business case and providing some solid momentum to take the model to a much larger scale. The approach also helps focus limited talent and resources. For example, if you only have a few of those precious data strategists, this approach gives you and them a chance to apply their magic to very real and specific business opportunities without burning them out and spreading them too thin across too many projects.

The secondary stage in structural change represents a more formalized statement of intent from the business that this impending change is real, proven, embraced, and will now be rolled out across the organization. In short, the new model will now be "institutionalized," typically through centers of excellence or other hubs that are developed in key parts of the world to help marketing teams make the big shift. These hubs are often the mission control centers discussed in chapter 7. In short, they are a physical embodiment of the new way of working. However, these hubs are not just for show but are also places for channeling and managing and visualizing data. In the process, marketers can make sure that security measures and various reporting lenses are in place to avoid any data scares, such as sensitive customer data inadvertently getting lost or distributed. The hubs are perfect locations for scaling data and digital talent, enabling the talent to learn valuable skills from each other that can then later be integrated into the larger marketing teams. Teams outside the center of excellence can tap into the hub's expertise on an as-needed basis without bearing the full burden of hiring someone and making other required investments. Furthermore, teams can also volunteer some of their own staff, full-time or part-time in the center of excellence to train them when the company is not able to hire someone. If you have a CDO, he or she may be based in these hubs. Nestlé's DAT facility is a perfect example of such an institutionalized model.

The benefits of the institutionalized model lie in its ability to very quickly scale a repeatable best practice model across teams and geographies. In addition, it maximizes the use of limited human resources, particularly the scarce digital and data talent everyone is searching for. In fact, this model enables that scarce talent to quickly attract and/ or train new talent. Finally, it helps to quickly build the foundational infrastructure, the adaptive marketing engine, across teams and geographies in a secure way that tests its ability to work under various scenarios. The only downside is that it doesn't build an adaptive approach into every team.

And this brings us to the final model. The "integrated" model represents a more mature stage of adaptive evolution when most teams are equipped with the knowledge, tools, and resources to become truly adaptive. For example, every team may have its own personalized reporting system, streaming real-time data to personal devices for instant analysis. Mission control rooms will be routinely used by the team to make quick, agile decisions, and programmatic solutions and algorithms will do the same through automation. Cross-functional thinking and coordination will become second nature, particularly when it comes to interpreting new data trends. Talent, such as digital analysts, will normally form a core part of the team. All the enterprise technology required will be implemented and accessible and routinely used.

To be clear, in this new integrated model, not every team will have everything. For example, the centers of excellence with its mission control room and data scientists may be shared across teams rather than built into every function. Data management services and application development could stay centralized for economies of scale. Jaguar Land Rover has taken this approach under Nathan Summers. "The Enterprise on Star Trek needs a lot of people analyzing and acting on a lot of data to function," says Summers, "but it doesn't need a dozen different engineer rooms. One Scotty is enough."

The one constant danger of any integrated model is that it begins to lose its edge. By normalizing the change, the organization ironically may become complacent, not constantly refining or challenging the system to adapt to become better, smarter, faster. Companies need to keep some mechanism in place to avoid this complacency. Often the CDO will be positioned as a disruptive force, constantly repeating the life cycle of the "incubate, institutionalize, integrate" model. New tests need to be explored, new data sourced, new learning codified, new training introduced, new technology layered into the mix. This, to paraphrase Elton John, is the adaptive circle of life.

Top Tips for Structuring for Adaptive Marketing

1. One size does not fit all. Different organizations in different markets with different stages of digital and data maturity will require different structural models. Assess your options and what will work best for your company. Be adaptive when it comes to your own structure.
2. Beware of politics. Once the organization rallies around the vision and ambition, everyone will want to "own" it. It must be a collaborative process to succeed, with multiple stakeholders supporting each other. Adaptive marketing is not about creating new silos.
3. Consider an initial test and/or center of excellence. Establish what good looks like to the organization, and use centers of excellence or hubs to create and scale repeatable models, nurture and train talent, and lay down the infrastructure required to benefit everyone.

4. Explore what should be centralized. Some elements of your adaptive structure should be centralized. There's no need for every team to have every component of the adaptive structure. Some resources are better shared for economies of scale, affordability, and even security.

5. Keep adapting. Once you've normalized your adaptive model, you'll need to keep adapting to keep it competitive and on top of the latest developments. Use an ongoing adaptive hub and "matrixed" reporting models to keep the company at the forefront.

In and Out

Of course, sometimes even with all the new talent and the new structure implemented, you will still need to move faster than perhaps your organization can currently handle. Sometimes that speed can be gained by simple changes to team structure. For example, Amazon drives agility and speed in its business by limiting the size of teams to eight to ten people, appropriately called "two-pizza" teams as the talent involved is the equivalent to the number of individuals who can be fed easily by two large pizzas. Amazon claims that these "two-pizza" teams are simply more efficient. For example, they move faster, are less likely to require status update meetings, and normally have much greater focus on singular tasks. Werner Vogel, CTO (Chief Technology Officer) of Amazon, claims that this decentralized structure results in a continuous stream of new services or products that can be brought to market in 10–15 days.

Google takes another approach when it comes to squeezing faster innovation out of its teams. Naturally, the teams have Google X, the company's semisecret facility led by Astro Teller, the grandson of Edward Teller, who is also known as the father of the hydrogen bomb. Astro and his team of wunderkinder are conjuring up all kinds of "moonshots," everything from artificial intelligence to autonomous cars. However, even though not everyone works in X and not everyone is a rocket scientist, Google still expects all of its engineers to think about innovation. They may work on smaller changes and ideas, call them "cloudshots," but this fresh thinking is still a vital way to keep the company evolving and ahead of the competition. Google's ITO (Innovation Time Out), or 80/20 model, encourages every Google engineer to spend one day a week, or 20 percent of his or her time, on "innovation" activities, which can be anything the employee finds stimulating or interesting. Numerous Google products and enhancements have come from the program, including everything from Gmail to Google News to AdSense.

However, if even after all the pizza team structures, moonshots, and ITO policies, you're still looking for more speed, an "open-sourced" approach to sourcing ideas, talent, and technology may do the trick. For example, Unilever has established its Foundry initiative in an effort to rapidly source new marketing ideas from external companies, ideas that perhaps it wouldn't normally get from within the company or its existing partner ecosystem. According to Unilever's Keith Weed, "one of the Foundry's main function is to cut out the complexity of doing business with a company of our size."

Start-ups are invited to pitch ideas to a Unilever brand, with winners receiving $50,000 in free funding to take the pilot to the next stage. Unilever also provides these start-ups with coaching on marketing to help them succeed. Weed believes that there have also been many intangible benefits as well. "The program has pushed our marketers to think more innovatively and iteratively," says Weed.

Kimberly-Clark takes a similar approach with its Innovation Lab event held each year at the Consumer Electronics Show in Las Vegas. The company issues several brand challenges to the start-up community, reviews hundreds of ideas that are submitted, and then invites a few of the best companies to pitch those ideas in person to a cross-functional senior management team during the CES conference each January. Several winners are selected, and then progress into a much deeper discussion about bringing ideas to life as well as investment. Netflix held a similar contest and went so far as to offer $1 million to anyone who could significantly improve the company's movie recommendation system.

Other companies have actually opened up outposts in Silicon Valley and other entrepreneurial locations in order to tap into the talent, culture, and wider innovation ecosystem that tends to develop in those locations. Nestlé opened up its Silicon Valley outpost in 2013, and its team on the ground in California routinely plugs hot new start-ups back into its business all around the world. Walmart actually bought a Silicon Valley start-up called Kosmix in order to bring in new talent residing in this heartland of innovation. Kosmix has since been rebranded as Walmart Labs. However, everything else has intentionally stayed the same; Kosmix's original start-up mentality remains impervious to Walmart's relatively more traditional corporate culture. Walmart Labs continues to attract great entrepreneurial talent, people who are focused on driving rapid innovation, particularly in the mobile space.

Leave it to Tesla founder Elon Musk to find an even more ambitious "open-source" path to driving innovation in his company. In June 2014, Tesla essentially ripped up all of its technology patents and gave away most of its company secrets for free in the hopes of bringing in new talent and ideas to further revolutionize electric cars and the broader electric transportation ecosystem. It was an audacious gamble on Musk's part, one perfectly aligned with his bigger and just as audacious ambitions to turn the existing fossil-fuel based transportation system upside down and drive it out of business. In short, Tesla wasn't competing with other electric cars, it was competing with the entire gasoline-guzzling car industry. If the overall electric car ecosystem advances and more people buy more electric cars, then Tesla and its broader vision will be victorious. Tesla thus created one giant automotive hackathon where anybody and anyone could play with Tesla technology and code to try and advance the overall cause.

The jury is still out on whether Tesla and its patent-free approach will move people from gasoline cars to electric cars. Nevertheless, the learning from Musk, Unilever, Nestlé, Kimberly-Clark, and many others is that in the race to win, companies are not frightened to adapt their own structures to make them much more open to other companies and outside talent.

Top Tips for Opening Up

1. Add speed and innovation to your own teams. Explore simple team structures, tactics, and heuristics to encourage quicker decision making and greater innovation.
2. Tap into start-ups. Consider establishing more formalized methods to tap into the start-up community for more ideas and talent. Determine the value exchange, for example, their ideas in return for investment or coaching.
3. Create an innovation hub. Explore opening up an innovation hub, particularly in destinations known as innovation hotbeds like Silicon Valley, Shoreditch, and Shenzhen.
4. Hold a hackathon. An increasingly popular method to bring together internal and external talent to conjure up and code ideas around business challenges in a very short time.
5. Go really open. Consider lifting the hood on your patents and intellectual property in order to mobilize more talent and companies to rally around a broader cause that benefits them and you.

Drinking the Kool-Aid

Another recurring theme from many adaptive marketing leaders is their reliance on key partnerships to help them change and mobilize their own company. "One of the first things we did was to create big partnerships with the likes of Google and Facebook," says Unilever's Keith Weed. "While we are not the biggest advertisers with them, we try to leverage their ecosystem more than others, particularly with innovation. We want to get to the future first."

Weed, along with Nestlé's Tom Buday, were both founding members on Facebook's Marketing Council, which consists of a little over a dozen of the industry's top marketing executives. The Facebook Marketing Council helps advise Facebook management on everything from its brand positioning to its ad product road map, and in return council members typically get a first look at beta opportunities and innovations.

However, marketers like Unilever and Nestlé are "leaning in" to Facebook and others like Google for more than just new advertising opportunities. In many respects, they are plugging into those companies and their highly disruptive cultures, particularly their almost pathological need for innovation and their fast-moving, iterative approach to doing things. "Fail fast" are arguably the two most commonly mentioned words in Silicon Valley. It's almost like every resident in the Bay area has drank out of a large vat of "fail fast" Kool-Aid. It's both contagious and liberating once you take a sip.

Weed and his peers at other companies are trying to channel that "fail fast" Kool-Aid and its unique cultural energy and behavior into their own companies, from the very top of the organization to the rank and file, from the United States to around the world, from the marketing departments to the technology teams. And in many cases this is desperately needed, for more than anything else adaptive marketing is an attitude, a set of personal behaviors that build up to a broader corporate culture that embraces a restlessness to quickly drive change, to openly collaborate with others, to personally knock down the barriers that so many data hoarders create in their quest to be the exclusive holders of knowledge and presumably of power.

Fear is one of the greatest barriers to that adaptive mentality. For many organizations, and indeed cultures, there is still a real stigma to failure, and changing that is not an easy thing. As mentioned above, frequently this new culture and acceptance of failure, as long as it's fast and informed, must start with the leadership in the company. It's the leader in the end who establishes acceptable behavior: the pace of everyday work, the appetite for risk, and the camaraderie among peers and employees. Arguably, this is why so many founders of start-ups are the most shining examples of adaptive and innovative cultures: Steve Jobs, Larry Page, Elon Musk, Mark Zuckerberg, to name only a few.

Older more traditional companies often find it hard to shake up long-established slow and conservative cultures. Which is why many of them take a pilgrimage to what has become the marketing industry's version of a holy site. Silicon Valley routinely sees dozens of corporate board room and marketing teams making their way to northern California to see this hotbed of adaptive marketing and rapid innovation firsthand. This has become such a phenomenon that companies have had to adapt their physical structures to compensate for the influx of visitors. "We had to construct a new building called the Partner Plex just to handle the visitors," says Google's Eileen Naughton.

Massive German publisher Axel Springer needed a shake-up. Springer CEO Matias Dopfner decided to create a "Visiting Fellows" program as the catalyst behind this much needed cultural change. Dopfner sent his senior management team to Silicon Valley to experience firsthand the entrepreneurial fast-paced culture that pervades the area. Springer executives visited Google, eBay, Facebook, and assorted start-up hubs, learning about their approach to work and the environments that their employees find most collaborative and productive. Everything from open-seating plans to standing-only meeting rooms to free cafeterias to meditation rooms was on the agenda. However, Dopfner also decided to get his executives out of their comfort zone. So he forced them to share rooms together, in some cases even the same bed, albeit king-size beds. It was all very rock n' roll and California for these traditional German executives.

The program was an instant success, and while Axel Springer hasn't turned into Google overnight, the nearly 70-year-old traditional German company was suddenly galvanized to become a much more agile, digitally focused organization. As a result, Springer has made significant inroads into the digital advertising business, which is an essential adaption for any newspaper. By 2014, Axel Springer had positive performance of its digital activities in all three operating segments, which offset the lower revenues in the traditional print business. In fact, for the first time ever, Axel Springer's digital media accounted for more than half of total revenues on a pro-forma basis.

The "Visiting Fellows" program has continued and expanded to include more employees at all levels of the organization who will remain in Palo Alto for a period of three to six months. These fellows will be given a reprieve from their existing duties while others back home pick up the workload.

While not a cure-all, tapping into the raw energy and ethos via partnerships is yet another means to help inspire as well as transform your company faster than perhaps you could do on your own. Go ahead, drink the Kool Aid.

In this chapter we explored the light touch required to turn your company into a faster, data-friendly, innovative company. That touch must start from the top of the organization in order to succeed. Without clear leadership and a clear vision, adaptive marketing will struggle to ever become a fundamental way of working throughout the business. While old talent, particularly the lost generation, can sometimes be retrained, new talent will be needed at the top and the bottom of the organization. Different structures can be adopted and adapted based on different circumstances, and an open approach is becoming more prevalent in order to tap into new talent and ideas faster than ever before.

In our next chapter we will get a glimpse into the future to explore what adaptive marketing may or may not look like in a much more hyperconnected world. Hold on to your seat.

Top Tips for Developing an Adaptive Structure

1. Lead from the front. Leadership is fundamental for success. Set a vision and walk the talk. Don't be frightened to adapt your plan as you go along.
2. Train or find the right people. Explore training programs to upskill your talent, but recognize you will most likely need to bring in new talent, particularly people with data skills.
3. Consider a CDO. Given the rifts and tensions between CMOs and CIOs, a Chief Data or Chief Digital may help build bridges and ensure a connected approach in the organization.
4. Be open. Assess opportunities to tap into more talent and ideas faster via innovation labs or start-up sourcing efforts.
5. Leverage partnerships. Establish key partnerships with companies that can help inspire your people, including senior management, and share some of its cultural and behavioral DNA.

CHAPTER 7.1

The Weather Man on Data

Curt Hecht
Chief Global Revenue Officer
The Weather Channel

Every quarter, businesses report their earnings, and frequently losses are attributed to weather conditions—that it reduced foot traffic or the need for certain products. In fact, one third of the economy of the United States is impacted by weather, for a total of $580 million each year.[10]

The Weather Company recognized that it could help marketers not only to reduce the weather's negative impact on sales, but in fact help them to leverage weather conditions—both good and bad—to their advantage and actually increase sales. The company could do this by leveraging its immense trove of historical weather data, weather forecast data, and location data to create weather-triggered messaging. Where available, the Weather Company would marry that data with retail sales data to create predictive marketing strategies for advertisers.

For this undertaking, the Weather Company launched its WeatherFX division in 2012 to amass a group of meteorologists, data scientists, data analysts, engineers, and digital marketing experts to look under the hood and see all of the data the company had at its disposal and what insights could be culled from this to create these predictive marketing capabilities.

The key to success, however, was going beyond the obvious insights to unearth correlations that the marketers couldn't make on their own. We could make ourselves extremely valuable partners if we could bring something to the table that the others didn't already have internally and that could take their marketing capabilities to a whole new level.

For example, if it's going to snow in Detroit, home improvement chains already know to put snow shovels and salt at the front of their stores, and clothing retailers know to put sweaters on sale, and automotive suppliers know to promote snow tires. However, do these same businesses know how less obvious factors, such as wind speed, cloud coverage, or dew point may impact their sales?

We know drugstores should put bug spray on sale when the dew point hits a certain point in Texas, because that's when insect eggs tend to hatch, and thus people need bug repellent.

We also know that different conditions at different times of year can contribute to sales. Through Weather's partnership with Unilever on its campaign for Vaseline, Weather was able to determine that the most effective triggers for lotion sales were cold temperatures, cold and windy conditions, heavy snow, or dryness in Chicago and New York. In springtime in Phoenix, abnormally high wind speed leads to lotion sales. However, in the fall in the same city, above-average temperatures will lead to a bump in sales.

We also know that different levers move the same product in different ways in different cities. Beer sales increase in Chicago when there are three consecutive days of below-average temperatures, and in New York City they increase when the temperature is above average. This is because in the summertime, temperature increase is significantly higher in Chicago compared to other seasons, and as a result, it needs to be relatively cooler. This highlights the importance of differences relative to each geolocation.

Additionally, during the summer in Atlanta, people don't buy any more beer than usual, regardless of temperature changes. Thus, the data can also be useful in telling marketers when to hold back on marketing and promotions.

Insights mined by the Weather Company also showed how consumers feel and react based on location and how "good" and "bad" weather is relative and highly localized. A 60-degree day in April feels very different to people in Tampa than it does to people in Boston. Rain in Los Angeles causes very different behavior than does rain in Seattle—what to wear, what food to eat (salad versus comfort food), the leisure activities someone chooses (or whether to just stay home), whether to drive or walk. And on and on.

That is, the data clearly shows that weather influences an enormous amount of people's daily decisions. When those insights are combined with the triggers to activate a brand's marketing campaigns at the right time, in the right place, and with the right message for that location—a hot drink versus a cold drink, with a coupon and map to the local Starbucks or Dunkin' Donuts—the result is a helpful message for a consumer, rather than an intrusion.

That's really the key to winning when it comes to advertising now. Consumers expect messages to be personally relevant to them. While marketers want to toe the fine line between personal relevance and the creep factor, the creep factor will become less and less relevant as people begin sharing more of their personal data. The wins far outweigh the downside when it comes to targeted messages.

Everyone wants to sell their products and services as much as possible. But data proves the saying, "Timing is everything." It's critical to ensure an advertising message is received with open arms and a receptive mind. But once marketers gather those insights and find those sweet spots, they are mining data gold.

CHAPTER 8

Through the Looking Glass

For most of this book we have focused on the present: how marketers are currently using data to adapt everything from product to pricing to promotions. We've also explored how top companies are building adaptive marketing engines to best harness, manage, and action the data flowing inside and outside their organization. Finally, we've looked at the cultural and talent changes required to activate all of that infrastructure, to get teams to start thinking and behaving in an adaptive way. In this chapter we quickly explore the key trends that are shaping the opportunities for adaptive marketers over the next few years. We take a quick look through the "adaptive looking glass" to see how real-time data will impact the relationship between brands and consumers in an increasingly hyperconnected and hyper-personalized world.

Full Moons and Fit Bodies

People have speculated for years whether a full moon leads to a sleepless night. Bleary-eyed employees will often ask each other "how did you sleep?" searching for validation that there is indeed some correlation between the moon's phases and sleep deprivation. Well, my Jawbone Up can now put the matter conclusively to rest.

For those who don't know the product Jawbone Up, it is an ingenious little wearable device, a souped-up wristband really, that keeps track of how many steps you've taken each day and also of your sleep patterns at night. Everything from motionless deep sleep to every toss and turn is recorded. And yes, according to my Jawbone Up, there is indeed a direct correlation between my sleepless nights and a full moon.

Of course, Jawbone Up is just one of many emerging digital fitness monitors. Millions of health enthusiasts are strapping on Fitbits, Fitbugs, and Withings wearable technology in an effort to get in better shape by counting calories, tracking steps, and monitoring sleep patterns. However, it isn't just fitness enthusiasts who are benefiting from the "quantifiable-self" bonanza. The Mimo Smart Baby Monitor performs similar health-related tracking functions for your infant. Mimo is a little wearable gizmo that slips on to your baby's pajamas and keeps track of all kinds of data, everything from your child's breathing to whether she has rolled over. Even your dog can join the new digital fitness craze: Tagg collars enable you to track your pet's activities, ensuring your dog is meeting his daily exercise goals before getting his nightly bone for an evening snack.

In fact, quantifying and assessing eating and drinking habits seems to be an emerging trend as people continue to focus on every biometric measure imaginable. Hapifork monitors how fast you eat and vibrates when you need to slow down to improve digestion. MIT Media Lab's Cheers LED ice cubes detect your alcohol consumption based on an accelerometer that keeps track of the number of sips you've had and a timer that helps guess your level of intoxication based on the time elapsed. The ice cubes change color based on your intake, with red indicating you've had too much, and green giving you the OK to party on. Vessyl, cofounded by Justin Lee and Jawbone designer Yves Behar, is an intelligent cup that detects and analyzes any liquid you put into it and reports back to your mobile phone on various data points, including sugar, fat, protein, sodium, and caffeine levels. Vessyl can distinguish between different types of soft drinks, even variations on your favorite Starbucks coffee, including whether you've splurged on holiday gingerbread or pumpkin latte. Vessyl checks your hydration levels and estimates your beverage needs. All of this may seem rather superfluous, except that according to the US National Health and Nutrition Examination Survey, beverages are your number one source of calories. In effect, all this data provides you with an invaluable source of information to help you meet your diet and health goals.

The world of wearable and quantifiable-self technology is not standing still (no pun intended) but is rapidly growing and evolving every year. In fact it's changing so fast many pundits believe today's technology will become rapidly antiquated as biometric sensors are embedded into your Apple Watch or your Ralph Lauren shirt. In effect, the technology becomes invisible to you while it constantly monitors the biometrics of your choice. For example, MC10's Biostamp is a tiny little Band-aid-like device roughly the size of just two postage stamps. This Biostamp can be attached to any part of your body to analyze and report on everything from your temperature to your heart's performance. All of which can be transferred back to you and shared with your doctors and your family. Proteus Digital Health is attempting to take things a step further. Proteus is experimenting with a tiny pill that when taken every day like a vitamin will provide a wide range of biometric data to help you better manage your fitness and health. These advancements will most likely make the Jawbones and Fitbits of the world feel like the Apple Newton or Google Glass of its time—great idea, just not really delivering on its full potential.

Every Breath You Take, Every Move You Make

Regardless of your views on the current state of fitness devices, according to CCS Insight's most recent forecast, the overall wearable technology category is expected to grow from 22 million shipments in 2014 to 135 million in 2018. CCS also predicts that wrist-worn devices will account for roughly 87 per cent of wearables to be shipped in 2018, comprising 68 million smartwatches and 50 million smart bands. All in all, 250 million wearables will be in use by 2018. That's a lot of devices producing a lot of biometric data (see Figure 8.1).[1] And this isn't just any data. Biometric data offers adaptive marketers a gold mine of data, particularly when it comes to beauty, food, beverages, or really

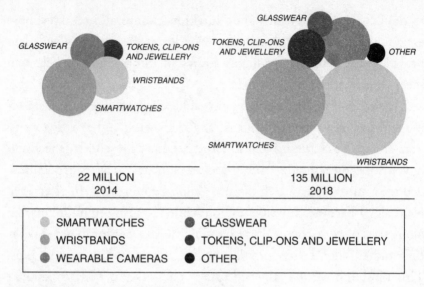

Figure 8.1 The Growth in Wearable Technology.
Source: CSS Insight, 2014.

any products or services that are dependent on consumers' physical condition.

Blood sugar levels too low? Why not take a break with KitKat? Need a meal that fits within your daily calorie limits? Here are some recipe suggestions from Unilever. Not enough sleep? Wake up with a special promotion from your local Starbucks. Full moon tonight? Best take some Nytol before going to bed.

Though wearable technology is still a nascent area, many companies are already exploring these types of scenarios. For example, mobile application Kiip aggregates your mobile behavioral data, including biometric information, into one destination and then provides brand-related rewards and content related to achievements and moments. So if you finish your daily exercise regime for the week, you may be rewarded with a free song from Nike or a discounted Magnum ice cream from Unilever.

UnderArmour's MapMyFitness also offers similar adaptive marketing opportunities for brands via what it calls "challenges." Coca-Cola sponsored one such challenge to MapMyFitness users. The "Take it to the Park" initiative was part of Coke's overall effort to fight obesity by encouraging more people to get out and get some exercise. The challenge invited consumers to take as many steps as they could in their local park. All of this biometric data was collected and geolocated, and the park that earned the most steps won the title "America's Favorite Park" as well a $100,000 recreation grant to build new fitness facilities and playground equipment.

In the future, pricing on some products may be variable depending on your biometric data. In effect, your body will indicate the potential demand for a certain type of food or beverage and once calibrated with supply, the price could be lowered or potentially increased based on that data. It's a tricky space that hasn't been fully defined yet. Nonetheless, some companies have already started experimenting with variable biometrics-based products and services.

For example, Apple recently announced a partnership with a company called Humana, which will enable people to share their Apple HealthKit data with the Vitality mobile application and in return get financial incentives for healthy behavior. For instance, if a consumer consistently meets her daily target of 10,000 steps, she may receive a discount on her monthly health care premium. This offers an intuitive and logical means for insurance companies to determine an individual's insurance costs by moving from a static, one-off medical evaluation to an ongoing health monitoring analysis: the healthier you behave, the lower your risk, and logically the lower your insurance costs. In fact, a recent survey of 900 adults in the United States revealed that nearly 60 percent of them would be more likely to use a fitness-tracking device if it meant possibly lower health insurance premiums.[2] Car drivers have already embraced a similar model in which usage-based real-time data determines the car insurance price. Progressive Insurance has led the way in using such adaptive pricing via its Snapshot in-vehicle monitoring devices.

Despite such precedents, the insurance industry hasn't yet taken a definitive stance on adaptive models based on biometric data. Currently, in the United States, the law allows health insurance companies to use wearable data for pricing only if this method is within the guidelines of the employee's wellness program. As a consequence, many companies are already using wearable biometric data from Jawbones and Fitbits to reward and incentivize their employees. This policy has worked to date given the nascent size of the wearable industry, but with millions of such devices and sensors about to enter the mainstream population, there will eventually be a need to get everyone aligned on the ethical boundaries of using biometric data, particularly as these devices become much more advanced and move into areas beyond steps and sleep patterns.

In fact, many analysts theorize that within the next few years the technology will have evolved sufficiently so that it will be able to warn individuals when they are about to have a heart attack or stroke. Described as a heart health game changer, Qardio is an existing suite of products that measures all the vitals for a healthy heart including blood pressure, heart rate, temperature, and activity. It also includes wearable ECGs and symptom trackers and allows the secure sharing of blood data with physicians and labs. It's not far-fetched to think that with a few simple predictive algorithms you could detect a conflux of data that would advise you to take an aspirin and get to the hospital now before your heart attack occurs. Perhaps Google's predictive engine Google Now will even automatically send for the ambulance to come pick you up.

Retailers are also tapping into wearable technology and biometric data to adapt the physical shopping experience. Boston's Innerscope Research uses glasses with a special camera to track eye movements and finger sensors to assess electricity levels on the skin. The data captured from this controlled research gives retailers invaluable insight into someone's neurological and physical reactions to the in-store experience. Innerscope has advised retailers on everything from the ideal level of sales signs to mannequin outfits to the best location of discounted products. In a future where such technology and sensors are regularly embedded into everyday clothes, including eye glasses, retailers may be able to get real-time data continuously, perhaps anonymized, that will help them adapt the store experience for the better.

For adaptive marketers, biometric information presents perhaps the ultimate adaptive messaging opportunity. Brand content, whether added-value health tips or simple promotions, can be personalized and customized to an unprecedented level of relevance to customers. Brand services could be triggered by the actual state of a person's health or by events that are predicted to happen in the near future. In any scenario, relevance will be essential, particularly given the personal nature of the data and devices. Think of it this way: advertising to consumers on the PC Internet is like taking them to the dance, advertising on a smartphone is like dating them, and advertising via wearable technology and biometric data is like sleeping with them. It's much more personal and therefore must be much more dependent on consumers opting in and giving permission to the brand to use the data and engage with them. As a consequence, brands that help or even entertain will be welcomed by consumers; annoying and interruptive ads will be filtered out of the ecosystem.

This sensitivity regarding health-related data is the reason why Apple is being so restrictive with HealthKit, its factory-installed fitness monitoring app, and third-party app extensions. According to Apple guidelines, "Apps may not use user data gathered from the HealthKit API for advertising or other use-based data mining purposes other than improving health, medical, and fitness management,or for the purpose of medical research."[3] Eventually Apple may find a way to loosen these restrictions, perhaps even to introduce iAds into the mix, but for now the company is proceeding carefully with biometric data.

Inverted Cyberspace

Wearable technology is just one sliver of the much broader Internet of Things. The next five years will be a veritable bonanza of everyday objects connected to the Internet. Cisco predicts that a total of about 50 billion "things" will join the Internet party over the next ten years. For many people the Internet will simply be built into almost everything around them.

William Gibson famously called it "inverted cyberspace," a world in which everything from your car to your hot tub will be connected to the Internet. Many people argue that in this hyperconnected future state the Internet will be so ubiquitous that most people won't realize they are connected. Logging on and accessing the Internet will become a thing your grandparents used to do. In the future, the Internet will simply be there all around you, and it will be fast; 5G Internet access will become the norm, which means that data will travel at speeds 1,000 times faster than today's 4G, which is at least ten times faster than 3G. While all this sounds like science fiction, anyone who has attended the annual Consumer Electronics Show in Las Vegas will know that most of this technology exists right now; it's just a question of cost-effectively scaling it and perfecting the user experience.

For example, homes will increasingly come with devices such as Google's Nest built into their structure. Nest is a new IP-enabled device that lets you remotely manage things like the temperature in your house, your smoke alarm, and your home security settings. Imagine never returning home from vacation to a cold house and having to endure a day wrapped in blankets waiting for the radiators to heat up. Instead, you can use Nest remotely to set the thermostat higher on the way home from the airport.

Your connected kitchen will include white goods, such as LG's Smart Fridge, which uses radio-frequency identification (RFID) technology to track and manage the foods it holds. RFID is already a well-established technology, which is estimated by IDTechEx to grow to over $30 billion in business by 2024.[4] The German government predicts the number of RFID tags in that country will go from today's 86 million to 23 billion by 2020.[5]

RFID chips are tiny tags that store data and enable objects to talk to each other. Hence, your refrigerator will be able to talk to the products stored in it, whether milk, yogurt, beer, or meat. With some chips able to communicate over a distance of hundreds of feet, your fridge could also assess any food in your kitchen, perhaps even foods in your neighbor's pantry. With one press on an application you could check which neighbors have some extra butter or eggs and then send a virtual request to borrow some if you need to.

For marketers there are multiple emerging adaptive opportunities within the broader Internet of Things landscape. Automatic replenishing of kitchen goods via home grocery delivery is one obvious example. Marketers could ensure their customers never run out of milk again. Even expiration dates could be factored into the equation, with reorders of everything from old eggs to expired allergy medication automatically put into your weekly shopping basket. The online grocery retailer Ocado in the United Kingdom has developed such a smart refrigerator that uses nano-tile shelving technology to move food around in the fridge, so food about to expire shortly is moved to the front rather than lingering in the back where it's quickly forgotten. Such continuous real-time data will give retailers and brands an opportunity to understand consumer demand at a previously unimaginable level. Essentially, marketers will be able to predict demand.

Other adaptive opportunities for marketers will include the ability to layer branded utilities and services on to connected devices and so essentially to become the apps consumers use most frequently for various needs. Recipe solutions is an obvious example. If RFID technology can assess the supply of available food in your kitchen, it could easily suggest doable recipes based on family members. IBM has developed Chef Watson, which experimented with just such technology and intelligence. Chef Watson is able to predict and cook dishes based on kitchen inventory, a total of 9,000 recipes from the magazine *Bon Appetit*, and some baked-in cooking rules.

When will such RFID-sensitive, IP-enabled machines and objects become the norm? The Smart Fridge has been around for years with limited success. As with many of these technologies, typically a number of factors must come together to suddenly push the new technology across the technology adoption chasm, as Geoffrey Moore famously called it. John Devlin, an RFID and NFC specialist with ABI Research in London, is on record as predicting that 2017–2018 will the time when smart fridges and other white goods begin to take hold among mainstream consumers in some markets. In an interview with *RFID Insider*, Devlin predicted the market will essentially double each year through 2017. "[With] domestic appliances alone (excluding CE), the market should increase about 14-fold from 2014 through 2018," claims Devlin.[6]

One of the major obstacles slowing down such adoption is the lack of common standards in the Internet of Things. This hyperconnected ecosystem will become really compelling to consumers when it seamlessly and invisibly communicates and shares data among its components. At the moment, many of these objects live in silos, performing useful functions on their own, but they are not nearly as intelligent and automated as we would want them to be. For consumers, this just means that the Samsung washing machine can't "talk" to the LG dryer. It's a big problem, and a few big companies are stepping up to solve it.

The Ecosystem Battles

Those big companies are the usual suspects, particularly Apple and Google, who are both developing common standards, albeit in wider closed ecosystems that still struggle to talk to each other. For example, Apple is making a strong play for the connected home with HomeKit, which is a technology for developers that allows you to control different objects from different manufacturers from one single device. Light dimmers, thermostats, garage door openers from totally different brands can all use HomeKit to hook up to the Apple ecosystem. Google has its own version called "Work with Nest."

Many marketers are exploring such nascent opportunities to create connected brand devices or service applications to be layered into this ecosystem. For example, recent "Work with Nest" partners include IP phone maker Ooma, which has developed a utility that automatically calls emergency services if your Nest smoke alarm goes off. Fan maker Big Ass Fans is also using Nest data to automatically adapt fan speeds based on thermostat readings to make for better temperature control. Such examples of "advertising so good it's a service" may represent the initial adaptive marketing opportunities for most brands—at least until market pressures force Google and others to open up the data for paid media and advertising sometime in the future.

Even Apple and Google's reluctance to allow health and home data to be used for advertising purposes has not stopped some companies from testing the waters. Mort Greenberg founded FitAd, a mobile and wearable advertising network based on a vision that most users wouldn't mind getting ads on wearable devices and Internet of Things objects and their associated apps if the ads were highly targeted and relevant. In short, with a true value exchange between consumer and brand, people would opt in. According to Greenberg, "App users can be further motivated with the right message from a brand. Place the wrong message, or, even worse, the wrong message from the wrong brand, and a user will quickly uninstall an app and never go back."[7]

Current FitAd clients, such as US train service Amtrak and running shoe HOKA ONE, are running ads within apps on everything from Sony to Samsung watches. The brands are seeking what Greenberg calls "Moments," which are triggered from data related to the Internet of Things and stored on mobile apps, including biometric data. "Moments can include beginning a run, descending a mountain, driving for your longest golf shot, beating your best 5k time," says Greenberg, "or simply making a healthy food or lifestyle choice that is being captured via an app or website." Brian Wong's Kiip takes a similar approach, and in its primary research has found that in addition to increasing excitement, such moment-based rewards also increased users' brand favorability, respect, and purchase intent by 10 percent compared to a negative 6 percent impact from simply running advertising. The data supports the notion that in this brave new hyperconnected world, marketers will need to put much greater focus on the value exchange or run the risk of simply annoying people.

Top Tips for Brands and the Internet of Things (IoT)

1. Determine the relevance. Wearables and IoT are poised for massive growth, but is it the right time for your target audience, your market, and your brand? Don't just jump on the bandwagon, assess when and if the IoT will be relevant for investment.
2. Define the value exchange. Think through the value exchange to discover what your customers really want from you. Why would they give you permission to engage? What will make them opt in?

3. You can't annoy people into liking you. Don't be tempted by every opportunity to bombard people with messages. Wearables and the IoT are not another place to dump your advertising. Avoid the mistakes of the past (for example, pop-up ads).

4. Think about services and utilities. How can IoT data, including biometric information, be used to improve the experience people have with a brand, particularly in physical places?

5. Explore your own IoT territory. Is there an opportunity on your own or with another company to develop your own wearable technology or IoT product or service? Is there a natural territory for your brand to extend itself?

Van Gogh's Ear

Dutch artist Vincent Van Gogh created dozens of masterpieces during his 37 years on this planet. Anyone who has visited the Van Gogh Museum in Amsterdam will have been dazzled by dozens of swirling sunflowers, portraits, and landscapes. But if you look closely at these paintings you can see signs of a tortured artist who battled anxiety and depression, which ultimately led to him cutting off his left ear in 1888 and to an early death.

German artist Diemut Strebe wanted to capture this conflicted part of the artist's psyche during a Van Gogh exhibition at the Center for Art and Media in Karlsruhe, Germany. Dozens of ideas came to mind, but it was only when he started experimenting with 3-D printing that he came up with a novel idea. Was there a way to use this new technology to somehow recreate Van Gogh's missing left ear?

Strebe tracked down some cells from the great-great-grandson of Van Gogh's brother, Theo, and when he combined these with some other DNA was able to grow a living replica of the ear via 3D technology. The ear was created using a 3D printer and was grown in Boston's Brigham and Women's Hospital. Said ear is apparently still alive thanks to nourishing fluids and may eventually make its way on a tour around the world.

Beyond body parts, 3D printing has emerged as one of the major new innovations in technology over the past few years. The annual

Consumer Electronics Show in Las Vegas is full of companies hawking their latest printers; while still bulky and unwieldy, these printers are beginning to drop in price and become more affordable to households. It remains to be seen whether 3D printers get widely embraced or become a niche product for the affluent and businesses.

Brooklyn-based MakerBot is one of the more serious contenders in the 3D printing sector. With over 600 employees, the company is quickly driving down prices on its product range and also helping both brands and consumers to tap into the full potential of 3D printing. Some companies have already dipped their toes into the water with MakerBot's support.

For example, Martha Stewart Living Omnimedia partnered with MakerBot to create a cobranded collection of kitchenware goods called the Trellis Collection. Now, consumers at home with a MakerBot printer and the proper material can create their own Martha Stewart product right in the kitchen. A variety of Martha's favorite designs and colors were made available, allowing budding artists to print everything from napkin rings to coasters. Additional cocreated designs are due to be released, enabling MakerBot owners to keep developing and adapting new products with the materials in their home without a trip to the shop or waiting for the Amazon package to arrive. It all sounds great, but the extensive safety notes clarifying that the items are not guaranteed to be safe for food or water or in the dishwasher or microwave may give pause to some.

However, 3D Ventures has no such qualms about eating the chocolate that gets printed from Candy, the first 3D confectionery printer in the world. The company currently sells two machines that make chocolate and sugar-based confectionery in various elaborate shapes and sizes and colors. Given its hefty price tag (at the time of writing roughly $5,000) the primary target audience for the machines consists mainly of small businesses, such as bakeries and restaurants, but over time, as prices drop, the machine could become a household staple for many chocoholics around the world. In addition, 3D Ventures has a mobile app called Digital Cookbook that guides consumers into creating their own computer-aided designs and chocolate treats. Candy is not the only 3D food printer on the market; competitors around the world include Foodini, Chefjet, and Choc Edge. This proves that if nothing else, the 3D printing industry can come up with some nifty product names.

For adaptive marketers, there are several potential opportunities, ranging from developing their own 3D printers to supplying the ingredients to those of others. For example, KitKat could provide branded chocolate capsules to enable consumers to create their own personally designed KitKat-shaped products. Or Nestlé could develop its own 3D printing range, a Nespresso-like suite of machines and ingredient capsules that consumers could use to create Nestlé confectionery.

Jay Rogers, CEO of Local Motors, has more ambitious plans for 3D printing. The company recently launched the world's first 3D printed electric car. The Strati took over four months to create, but Rogers believes that turnaround times could be 24 hours in the future as the 3D printing technology improves, a significant improvement in car delivery times over today's typical three-month wait. Of course, the Strati has only 49 parts compared to the 25,000 found in an average car, which means there is probably less adaptability in the features but certainly more agility in the turnaround time. Rogers plans to sell the cars at a price somewhere between $18,000 and $30,000 and to develop localized versions based on unique environmental conditions around the United States.

Clearly, 3D printing is a technology still in its very early stages. How the technology evolves and, more important, how consumers wish to use it, remains largely unknown, unless of course you need to grow your ear back.

Locking Up Your Data

The unfortunately named New York City mayoral candidate Anthony Weiner became an inspiration to comedians around the United States when the press revealed that he had an ongoing sexting issue. With his publically-humiliated wife standing by his side, Weiner apologized for his transgression and promised to seek professional help to overcome what he called an addiction. Several months later he was right back at it again, sending Weiner photos to a woman in Indiana. He didn't win the mayoral race.

What Weiner and his wife may not have realized is that sexting has moved beyond a niche activity to a mainstream phenomenon in many countries around the world. Nearly 25 percent of all respondents in the United States to a *Time* Mobility Poll—including a majority of men aged 18 to35—have sent a sexually provocative picture to a partner or loved one. Think that's bad? Try 45 percent of South Africans, 54 percent of Indians, and 64 percent of Brazilians.[8]

Whether you sext or not, most consumers are beginning to understand that they are leaving a trail of very personal data, some of it potentially embarrassing, in their digital exhaust. People do stupid things online, and those stupid things can easily get shared with many other people, perhaps in perpetuity. Add in health-related data, and you have a perfect storm of potential data issues.

Consumers are beginning to notice, perhaps spurred on by Edward Snowden's revelations in 2011 that various governments routinely collect and review personal Internet data, including Google and Yahoo data. According to the Centre for the Digital Future (CDF), 43 percent of Internet users are concerned with the government intruding on their online privacy. Unfortunately for marketers, that number climbs to 57 percent when it comes to corporations. In other words, people trust companies less than the government when it comes to snooping on their online data.[9]

Parents are increasingly worried about the data their children are leaving online. "This generation of parents has to tell their children five more things to watch out for than previous generations," says the CDF's Jeff Cole. "Spring break has become very tame because they've learned it will be on Facebook in 60 seconds."

While some people have argued that children will develop a new set of privacy values for the Internet age, e.g., "everyone is doing it mom," others like the CDF's Jeff Cole disagree. "We can see 15 years of change through our research," says Cole. "The former 15-year-olds who are now 30 care a lot about privacy. Once people get older, they care just as much about privacy as the previous generation. Your medical and financial history is not very interesting when you are young. That changes when you are 30."

The solution to all of these privacy and data issues may lie with consumers themselves. While still nascent, the concept of personal data lockers may gather momentum over the next few years. Data lockers are a virtual version of the physical form: a data locker is essentially a place to securely keep all of your stuff, a bit like today's cloud-based storage systems but on steroids.

Data lockers bring several benefits to consumers. First, consumers can not just add but also delete information as they please. According to Microsoft, 73 percent of people would be interested in a service that allows them to remove data.[10] The second benefit is potential profit from consumer data, basically by companies making money off packaging and selling consumer data for various purposes. This profit is estimated to reach around $1 trillion by 2020.[11] Many consumers wouldn't mind earning a small slice of that business. How exactly? Consumers could "sell" access to their personal data. In essence, it's a reversal of today's model where you generally get a free service in return for supplying your eyeballs and data, which in turn are used by publishers to sell advertising. It's perhaps one reason why a study of Dutch consumers commissioned by Qiy found that 80 percent of participants wanted to know more about their data and 85 percent wanted more control over their data.[12]

In a future where consumers store and manage their own data, they may grant publishers and brands permission to use their stored data and content for various purposes, including advertising, but on their terms. Consumers will create their own APIs that will distribute their data and content to various organizations, publishers, and brands with accompanying rules for usage. People will control who can advertise to them—content, services, applications—how, when, where, and on which destinations and devices in their personal connected ecosystem. So we may be moving from a world of business APIs (application programming interfaces) to a future of individual PAIs (personal accessible information).

Adaptive marketers also stand to benefit as well. First, with a proper value exchange you may be able to create a direct relationship with consumers and gain access to a rich data set that can be leveraged for everything from product development to advertising. According to eMarketer, 37 percent of today's web traffic stems from nonhumans, often technology used to index search results. A total of $6 billion in advertising fraud results from this traffic: essentially advertisers putting ads in front of nonexistent people on the Internet.[13] With personal data lockers you know there is a real person on the other end. Data lockers can give you a wealth of information on that individual; the lockers are essentially synchronized customer relationship management systems that enable you to adapt almost every element of your marketing to make it more relevant to customers.

So far, data lockers have not caught on widely. Several companies and initiatives have emerged in recent years, including the Locker Project, Datacoup, MyPermissions and Handshake, all with limited success. Of course, everything could change if the Googles and Facebooks of the world venture into the data locker territory; after all, they already have most of the world's data stored on their servers, but they don't have much of a vested interest in helping you to monetize your data given their reliance on advertising as their primary source of revenue.

Apple, Amazon, and Microsoft are arguably less dependent on advertising, which represents a tiny sliver of their overall businesses. Consequently, all three are in a much better position to offer such data locker services, which may help them undermine archenemies like Google. Even Apple CEO Tim Cook has reflected on the issue. Speaking at a Goldman Sachs conference in 2015, Cook said, "So we think over the arc of time, consumers will go with people they trust with their data. People are unknowingly sharing things with others, and info can be pieced together. Over time people will realize this more and demand privacy."[14]

Other businesses, particularly the telecom carriers, are also hovering over the space. Carriers are in an ideal solution because they supply the primary pipes that you use across multiple devices to exchange data on the Internet. Governments could also step in and drive a regulated solution. The government of the United Kingdom has introduced a voluntary program called Midata that enables consumers to get back their information from any company that has signed up, including Telefonica and the BBC. The government of the United States is currently rolling out numerous "button" initiatives that consolidate consumer data into single access points. For example, the recent "Green Button" initiative is forcing all utility companies across the country to provide consistent data and APIs to consumers to collect usage information for things such as water and gas. Likewise the "Blue Button," which does the same for health-related data. The "MyData Button" initiative does the same for tax-related data (leave it to the IRS to take the color out of the button). Perhaps in the future the button initiative will broaden to include and aggregate more data sets, which will make it easier for consumers to manage their data in one place—and for the US government to know what you are up to.

Hello HAL

Futurist Ray Kurzweil made some bold predictions in his 2005 book *The Singularity Is Near: When Humans Transcend Biology.* The singularity he refers to it is the hypothesis that by the year 2045 technology will advance to such a state that people will become one with machines, augmented by nanotechnologies and artificial intelligence. Essentially, you will live on in perpetuity in the form of robotics and data.

Ray now works at Google. Which may explain why the search and online video company has been making some pretty bold acquisitions over the last few years, including robotics and artificial intelligence companies Boston Dynamics, Schaft, and DeepMind. Somewhere deep in a secret lab right now, Ray and the rest of the Google X team are tinkering away at something that could be truly momentous.

At Deepmind, the company's Neural Turing Machine combines computer-processing with the human brain's learning ability, which enables the machine to program itself. In a nutshell, the machine combines the adaptive instincts of a human being with the processing power of a computer. It's not perfect yet, but this gives you some insight into Google's future ambitions. As Larry Page himself declared way back in 2002, "Google will fulfill its mission only when its search engine is AI-complete. You guys know what that means? That's artificial intelligence."

By 2045, marketers may be hardwired into artificial intelligence and neuroscience, a continuous loop of synchronized data resulting in an immersive adaptive experience constantly changing around you. In the meantime Google Now is already putting search one step ahead of a physical action. Such predictive technologies may be the first glimmer of artificial intelligence. It's like having HAL from *2001: A Space Odyssey* in your phone and rather than just responding to questions, actually predicting what you need.

If you believe Kurzweil, you won't even need to be physically alive by that time, as you can live on forever, bringing an entirely new meaning and calculation to customer lifetime value.

On the other hand, maybe people will just get tired of all of this connectivity and technology. Perhaps digital vacations and data bankruptcies will become increasingly common, as individuals duck out of the matrix and decide to remain anonymous or completely disconnect. The rise of social applications such as SnapChat and Whispr and search engines like DuckDuckGo indicate at least some interest in the anonymized platforms. Meanwhile, "digital detox" services and advice are becoming increasingly popular in some parts of the world. Digitaldetox. org reminds people to "look up" and helps them to regain control of their lives. The company offers Digital Detox retreats, described as "a mindfulness-based and psychological driven program with a handful of journals, yoga mats, arts and crafts, typewriters, and one agenda; disconnect to reconnect." Tom's shoes, Pandora, and VH-1 are just a few of the companies that have used Digital Detox's services.

In reality, it's difficult to know how much people will lean into or turn away from this future hyperconnected world. And who will be the main disruptors and leaders is also opaque, although we can speculate that with cash-rich Google developing autonomous cars and Apple supposedly doing the same, both will be around for some time. Beyond that the companies that will shape our future may or may not be the same ones we know today. However, what is clear is that the ones that learn to adapt, and to adapt quickly, have a much better chance in succeeding than those who don't. As England's Lord Nelson once said, "Time is everything. Five minutes makes the difference between victory and defeat."

Big data in all its shapes and sizes—swift, secure, synchronous, small, and smart—can provide that extra advantage to help you recognize and act on your customers' needs faster than your competition. McKinsey has quantified it already: companies that are more data driven are 5 percent more productive and 6 percent more profitable than other companies.[15] This is a useful statistic that just reinforces what every good marketer already instinctively knows: in our very Darwinian world, your company either learns to adapt fast, or it dies.

CHAPTER 8.1

The Innovator on Data

Brian Wong, Founder
Kiip

Biometrics refers to the measurement of body signals: including but not limited to changes in pulse, breath, gaze, and temperature. These signals are indicative of your mood. If you're suddenly scared, your pulse will quicken. If you're attracted to a person or a visual, your gaze will focus on the object of desire, causing your pupils to dilate.

Marketers have longed to understand audience reactions to ads. For decades, market research has been employed, plugging groups of people into various biometric devices to collect data. This process is typically expensive. After all, if you're spending a few million dollars on a Super Bowl commercial, it can't hurt to throw a few extra dollars in the bucket to learn how a test group will react to that ad.

With the advent of popular wearables, however, these experiments will soon be replicable anytime, anywhere. Now, fitness trackers can measure your pulse while you work out. In the future, there's nothing to stop trackers from measuring your heart's reaction while you're idle—say, when you're playing a mobile game and viewing its respective ads. This idea expands beyond fitness trackers to wearables like smartglasses and other connected home and car devices rapidly filling the consumer marketplace. Thus, adaptive marketers may be able to track your actions and reactions all the time.

One company looking toward the future of smarter, more effective advertising is Kiip. Kiip is a rewards start-up that discerns "achievement moments" in mobile games and apps. It recognizes when users are most engaged on their phones, such as after a completed workout in a fitness app. Users then serendipitously earn moment-based rewards from relevant brands, such as a free sample of Propel or a discount on Nike products. As a result, Kiip boasts high engagement rates and happy users.

To back up what the company already knew to be true, Kiip ran a study that recorded user biometrics during these achievement moments. Users demonstrated elevated excitement during achievement moments and even more excitement when they earned moment-based rewards—significantly more so than during traditional ads. When presented with moment-based rewards, users smiled, their hearts raced a little faster, their eyes focused on their phones intently. Kiip figured out a way to grab the attention of users when they were most involved and then switch this new, positive focus to branded content. In addition to increasing excitement, the study also demonstrated that moment-based rewards increased users' brand favorability, respect, and purchase intent dramatically.

This new wave of advertising inherently understands users' emotions. Through moment-based rewards, adaptive marketers can show content that gets audiences excited; something that intelligently analyzes their current wants and needs. For instance, if a smart washer notifies the members of a family that they're low on detergent, Tide can swoop in and offer a discount on a new bottle. Advertisers will have the ability to show consumers products and services that make their lives better; something they *want* to see. There will no longer be ads that make consumers cringe. Instead, consumers will see only content they're biologically guaranteed to love.

Kiip recognizes that with each new wearable, there's a new device-specific opportunity to reach consumers. To prepare, the company has begun expanding beyond mobile. Kiip now offers rewards for everyday driving moments through Mojio, a smart device that plugs into cars to monitor internal actions (like engine function) as well external properties (such as the nearest gas station). Kiip is also imagining what rewards will look like on a slew of upcoming wearables, enabling advertisers to reach users on devices that don't even have screens.

This approach to the Internet of Things era gives brands a unique advantage when advertising on connected devices. Imagine all the devices to which this can extend, all the moments when brands can fortify their relationships with consumers. Brands can produce content that saves the day, such as providing a sample of baby medicine to a mother who just learned through a temperature-monitoring smart pacifier that her child is sick. Brands can also swoop in during celebratory moments, such as when a runner crosses his or her 100th mile with a fitness tracker, and provide the person with relevant products to fuel his or her next run.

By predicting needs and monitoring reactions to ads, adaptive marketers can determine what garners the best response and optimize content as it happens. Kiip refers to this as "real-time needs addressing," and it's just the launching point of using biometrics to shape consumer satisfaction. As this new concept takes root, brands will see increased engagement, and ultimately, purchase intent.

The future of advertising on connected devices is closer than we think. With the right approach, it will be the turning point to create meaningful relationships between brands and their consumers.

Notes

1 A Few Words about Data

1. IDC and EMC (2014), http://www.emc.com/leadership/digital-universe/2014iview/executive-summary.htm (home page), date accessed October 10, 2014.
2. TechCrunch (August, 2010) Eric Schmidt: Every 2 Days We Create As Much Information As We Did Up To 2003, http://techcrunch.com/2010/08/04/schmidt-data/
3. Google YouTube, https://www.youtube.com/yt/press/en-GB/statistics.html, date accessed October 10, 2014.
4. Science Daily (2013), http://www.sciencedaily.com/releases/2013/05/130522085217.htm, date accessed October 12, 2014.
5. Internet Live Stats, http://www.internetlivestats.com/internet-users/, date accessed August 7, 2014.
6. Interview with Eileen Naughton by Norm Johnston (February 5, 2015).
7. ITU Statistics, http://www.itu.int/en/ITU-D/statistics/Pages/default.aspx (home page), date accessed October 14, 2014.
8. TNW China Internet Network Information Center (CNNIC), a state-affiliated research organization, has released its report on the development and spread of the Internet throughout China covering the first half of 2013, http://thenextweb.com/asia/2013/07/17/report-70-percent-of-first-time-internet-users-in-china-surf-the-web-on-a-mobile-device/, date accessed August 16, 2014.
9. V3.co.uk (July, 2011), Mobile devices to exceed global population by 2014 as Asia comes online, IMS World Market for Mobile Handsets report, http://www.v3.co.uk/v3-uk/news/2097428/cellular-devices-exceed-people-2014-analysts-predict.
10. Nielsen (January 24, 2014), http://www.nielsen.com/in/en/insights/reports/2014/unstoppable--smartphone-surge-in-india-continues.html.
11. The Economist (May 27, 2013), http://www.economist.com/blogs/economist-explains/2013/05/economist-explains-18.
12. Cisco Cisco Visual Networking Index (February 5, 2014), Global MobileData Traffic Forecast Update, 2013–2018, http://newsroom.cisco.com/release/1340551/Cisco-Visual-Networking-Index-Forecast-Projects-Nearly-_2.
13. Consumer Reports State of the Net survey (January 16–31, 2012) by the Consumer Reports National Research, date accessed September 2, 2014.
14. PC Advisor, http://www.pcadvisor.co.uk/news/security/102866/89-of-web-users-share-personal-data-online/, date accessed December 2, 2014.
15. OFCOM *The Communications Market Report* (August 7, 2014), http://stakeholders.ofcom.org.uk/binaries/research/cmr/cmr14/2014_UK_CMR.pdf, downloaded September 5, 2014.

16. Microsoft (2010), Cross-Tab Online Reputation in a Connected World 2010, date accessed October 7, 2014.
17. Hytrust, http://www.hytrust.com/, date accessed October 6, 2014.
18. EMC sponsored IDC Digital Universe (2012), http://www.emc.com/collateral/analyst-reports/idc-digital-universe-united-states.pdf, downloaded December 6, 2014.
19. Customer CEO (2013), http://customerceobook.com/tag/jack-welch/
20. eConsultancy and Adobe Quarterly Digital Intelligence Briefing, Digital Trends 2015, date accessed February 2, 2015.
21. Wikipedia, http://en.wikipedia.org/wiki/Eastman_Kodak, date accessed February 2, 2015
22. BBC (2012), Can a Company Live Forever, http://www.bbc.co.uk/news/business-16611040, date accessed October 8, 2014.
23. EMC IDC Digital Universe (2012), New Digital Universe Study Reveals Big Data Gap: Less Than 1 percent of World's Data is Analyzed; Less Than 20 percent is Protected, http://www.emc.com/about/news/press/2012/20121211-01.htm, date accessed November 12, 2014.
24. Dan Ariely, Facebook, https://www.facebook.com/dan.ariely/posts/904383595868
25. Charles Duhigg, *The Power of Habit*, http://charlesduhigg.com/the-power-of-habit/

2   The World's Largest Focus Group

1. Coca-Cola (October 16, 2012), Everything You Need to Know About Coca-Cola Freestyle, http://www.coca-colacompany.com/stories/everything-you-need-to-know-about-coca-cola-freestyle.
2. *Social Times* (July11, 2014), Facebook Outperforms Twitter, Google+ Social Brand Interactions, http://www.adweek.com/socialtimes/social-brand-interactions/499952.
3. Nielsen Social (July 14, 2014), Connecting with Social Brand Ambassadors, http://www.nielsen.com/us/en/insights/news/2014/connecting-with-social-brand-ambassadors.html.
4. Interview with Chris Whalen by Norm Johnston (January 5, 2015).
5. *The Betterific Blog* (March 25, 2014), Starbuck's Crowdsourcing Success, http://blog.betterific.com/tag/my-starbucks-idea-anniversary/.
6. My Starbucks Idea, by Starbucks, http://mystarbucksidea.force.com/, downloaded January 30, 2015.
7. Lego Ideas, by Lego, https://ideas.lego.com/, downloaded January 26, 2015.
8. Nielsen (2013), The Mobile Consumer, http://www.nielsen.com/content/dam/corporate/uk/en/documents/Mobile-Consumer-Report-2013.pdf.
9. Bain (2013), Making it Personal: Rules For Success In Personalisation, http://www.bain.com/publications/articles/making-it-personal-rules-for-success-in-product-customization.aspx, downloaded July 8, 2014.
10. Mattel (October 16, 2013), Mattel Reports Third Quarter 2013 Financial Results and Declares Fourth Quarter Dividend, http://news.mattel.com/News/Mattel-Reports-Third-Quarter-2013-Financial-Results-and-Declares-Fourth-Quarter-Dividend-172.aspx.
11. *Mashable* (April 18, 2014), Social Seating Can Lead to Business Opportunities on Dutch Airline, http://mashable.com/2014/04/18/meet-seat-klm/.
12. *Make-Up Artist Magazine* (September 18, 2009) Estée Lauder Sacks Prescriptives, https://makeupmag.com/estee-lauder-sacks-prescriptives-2/
13. *The Marketing Engine*, (June 4, 2014), How to Innovate in Marketing, https://themarketingengine.wordpress.com/category/innovation/page/4/

3 #HappyCustomers

1. Neurosense, The Science of Good Service (September 2013) *American Express Service Study,* http://www.neurosense.com/index.php/en/media-news/interviews-and-tv-programs/323-amex-good-service.

2. Accenture 2013 Global Consumer Pulse Survey, http://www.accenture.com/SiteCollectionDocuments/PDF/Accenture-Global-Consumer-Pulse-Research-Study-2013-Key-Findings.pdf, downloaded November 4, 2014.

3. J. Allen, F. F. Reichheld, B. Hamilton, and R. Markey (2005), Bain: Closing the delivery gap.

4. Maritz Research and Evolve24: Twitter Study (September 2011), http://www.maritz-research.com/~/media/Files/MaritzResearch/e24/ExecutiveSummaryTwitterPoll.ashx, downloaded January 7, 2015.

5. Convince and Convert, 42 Percent of Consumers Complaining in Social Media Expect 60 Minute Response Time, http://www.convinceandconvert.com/social-media-research/42-percent-of-consumers-complaining-in-social-media-expect-60-minute-response-time/, date accessed November 7, 2014.

6. Lithium Millward Brown (October 29, 2013), Consumers Will Punish Brands that Fail to Respond Quickly on Twitter, http://www.lithium.com/company/news-room/press-releases/2013/consumers-will-punish-brands-that-fail-to-respond-on-twitter-quickly.

7. IPA (2014) #IPASocialWorks, Measuring Not Counting: Evaluating Social Marketing Communications, http://newmr.org/wp-content/uploads/sites/2/2014/10/Guide-to-Evaluating-Social.pdf.

8. Best Buy Geed Squad, http://www.geeksquad.com/careers/

9. *Econsultancy Blog* (August 28, 2013), Almost a Quarter of Business don't carry out any Relationship Marketing, https://econsultancy.com/blog/63303-almost-a-quarter-of-businesses-don-t-carry-out-any-relationship-marketing-report/.

10. *Synapse.Blog* (September 11, 2012), How Do you Value Your Brand's Social Connections, http://www.syncapse.com/how-do-you-value-your-brands-social-connections/#.VQLlwI7kdcQ, date accessed January 5, 2015.

11. *TNS Digital Life*, Understating the Opportunity For Growth Online (2011) http://static.tnsdigitallife.com/files/Digital_Life.pdf, downloaded October 7, 2014.

12. *The Huffington Post* (September 26, 2013), Barilla Pasta Won't Feature Gay Families In Ads, Says Critics Can 'Eat Another Brand Of Pasta', http://www.huffingtonpost.com/2013/09/26/barilla-pasta-anti-gay_n_3995679.html

13. *429* (September 30, 2013), Buitoni seizes opportunity to show support for LGBT customers: "Pasta for all", http://dot429.com/articles/3130-buitoni-seizes-opportunity-to-show-support-for-lgbt-customers-pasta-for-all

14. Ad Week (September 9, 2014), DiGiorno Is Really, Really Sorry About Its Tweet Accidentally Making Light of Domestic Violence Reminder to always check the context on hashtags, http://www.adweek.com/adfreak/digiorno-really-really-sorry-about-its-tweet-accidentally-making-light-domestic-violence-159998

15. Hellobee (April 3, 2014), MLB Player gets grief for taking paternity leave, http://boards.hellobee.com/topic/mlb-player-gets-grief-for-taking-paternity-leave

16. InContact (September 9, 2013), US Consumers Want Today's Companies to be Proactive in Customer Service, http://www.incontact.co.uk/call-center-industy-news/us-consumers-want-todays-companies-be-proactive-customer-service.

17. Forrester's Top Trends For Customer Service In 2014 (January 13, 2014), http://blogs.forrester.com/kate_leggett/14-01-13 forresters_top_trends_for_customer_service_in_2014.

18. Social Bro (Octonber 1, 2014), Xbox: What You Can Learn From The Most Responsive Brand On Twitter, http://www.socialbro.com/blog/xbox-what-you-can-learn-from-the-most-responsive-brand-on-customer-support-twitter

19. IPA (2014) #IPASocialWorks Measuring Not Counting: Evaluating Social Marketing Communications, http://newmr.org/wp-content/uploads/sites/2/2014/10/Guide-to-Evaluating-Social.pdf.

4 Exploring the Spectrum

1. Interview with Rob Norman by Norm Johnston (January 5, 2015).

2. Neilsen (February 2014), The Digital Consumer, http://www.slideshare.net/tinhanhvy/the-digital-consumer-report-2014-nielsen, date accessed September 17, 2014.

3. Kantar (TMS) (10 July 2014), TV Strikes Back: Rise of Digital Devices Drives new Viewing Habits, http://www.tnsglobal.com/press-release/connected-life-tv-press-release.

4. BGR (February 2013). Smart TV Sales Soared in 2012, Set Do dominate TV Market by 2015, http://bgr.com/2013/02/22/smart-tv-sales-2012-340405/.

5. 2013 Strategy Analytics' Smart TV Forecast (2013), https://www.strategyanalytics.com/default.aspx?mod=pressreleaseviewer&a0=5472, date accessed December 12, 2014.

6. eMarketer Key Digital Trends for 2014, http://www.slideshare.net/ElenaPikunova/e-marketer-keydigitaltrendsfor2014, date accessed December 13, 2014.

7. eMarketer (October 2014) 2014 Programmatic Advertising Forecast, http://www.marketingmobile.co/wpcontent/uploads/2014/10/eMarketer_2014_Programmatic_Advertising_Forecast-Digital_Display_Spending_Broadening_Beyond_Open_Exc....pdf, downloaded December 12, 2014.

8. Interview with Keith Weed by Norm Johnston (February 4, 2015).

9. Interview with Luis di Como by Norm Johnston (February 4, 2015).

10. Thinkbox, Mediacom, Discover the Power of TV Advertising, http://www.thinkbox.tv/discover-the-power-of-tv-advertising/.

11. *Harvard Business Review* (January 31, 2014), Research Shows Which Ads are likely to Make Multitaskers Buy, https://hbr.org/2014/01/research-shows-which-tv-ads-are-likely-to-make-multitaskersbuy/?utm_source=feedburner&utm_medium=feed&utm_campaign=Feed%253A+harvardbusiness+%2528HBR.org%2529.

12. Civic Science: Resource Library, http://civicscience.com/library/, downloaded February 2, 2014.

13. Interview with Pete Blackshaw by Norm Johnston (January, 2015).

14. Interview with Eric Frankel by Norm Johnston (January, 2015).

15. Choicestream (September 18, 2014) Dear [First Name]. Are you missing out on TRULY personalized Email?! http://www.choicestream.com/2012/09/18/dear-are-you-missing-out-on-truly-personalized-email/.

5 Blurred Lines

1. Interview with Barry Kahn by Norm Johnston (January, 2015).

2. Cheap Air.com (April 2014), When Should You Buy Your Airline Ticket? Here's What Our Data Has to Say, http://www.cheapair.com/blog/travel-tips/when-should-you-buy-your-airline-ticket-heres-what-our-data-has-to-say/, date accessed September 3, 2014.

3. *Wall Street Journal* (August 23, 2012), On Orbitz, Mac Users Steered to Pricier Hotels, http://www.wsj.com/articles/SB10001424052702304458604577488822667325882.

4. *Wall Street Journal* (December 24, 2012), Websites Vary Prices, Deals Based on Users' Information, http://www.wsj.com/articles/SB10001424127887323777204578189391813881534.

5. J. Turow, L. Feldman, and K. Meltzer (2005), Open to Exploitation: America's Shoppers Online and Offline, date accessed December 3, 2014.

6. *ABC News* (September 29, 2000), Amazon Error May End "Dynamic Pricing," http://abcnews.go.com/Technology/story?id=119399, date accessed September 3, 2014.

7. eMarketer (July 23, 2014), Worldwide Ecommerce Sales to Increase Nearly 20 percent in 2014, http://www.emarketer.com/Article/Worldwide-Ecommerce-Sales-Increase-Nearly-20-2014/1011039#sthash.DXhZil72.dpuf.

8. GroupM (2014), GroupM Interaction 2014, http://www.groupmpublications.com/Interaction-2014-4.htm.

9. The Digital Future Project (2013), Surveying The Digital Future Year Eleven, http://www.digitalcenter.org/wp-content/uploads/2013/06/2013-Report.pdf (home page), date accessed February 3, 2015.

10. eMarketer (December 2014), What's Mobile's Role in the Omnichannel Experience? Mobile is Often the Catalyst For sales, http://www.emarketer.com/Article/Whats-Mobiles-Role-Omnichannel-Experience/1011737#sthash.J3ON760Z.dpuf.

11. Nielsen (February 2013), The Mobile Consumer: A Global Snapshot, http://www.nielsen.com/content/dam/corporate/uk/en/documents/Mobile-Consumer-Report-2013.pdf, downloaded January 6, 2015.

12. Internet Retailer (September 26, 2011), Shopkick Users a Curious Bunch, https://www.internetretailer.com/2011/09/26/shopkick-users-curious-bunch.

13. POPAI, The Global Association For Marketing At Retail (May 2012), Shopper Engagement Study, http://www.popai.fr/textes/Shopper_Engagement_Study.pdf, downloaded September 4, 2014.

14. Marketing Sherpa (October 23, 2012), Marketing Research Chart Average Website Conversion Rates, by Industry, http://www.marketingsherpa.com/article/chart/average-website-conversion-rates-industry.

15. Nielsen (February 24, 2014), How Smartphones are Changing Consumers' Daily Routines Around the Globe, http://www.nielsen.com/us/en/insights/news/2014/how-smartphones-are-changing-consumers-daily-routines-around-the-globe.html.

16. InMarket, http://www.inmarket.com, (home page), date accessed February 2, 2014.

17. Interview with Preston Reed by Norm Johnston (January 5, 2015).

18. Interview with Jeff Cole by Norm Johnston (January 8, 2015).

6 Heavy Lifting

1. CompTIA (September 2013), Big Data Insights and Opportunities, http://www.comptia.org/.

2. Interview wit Nathan Summers by Norm Johnston (February 11, 2015).

3. Mastering Adaptive Customer Engagements: A Look Into How Today's Marketing Leaders Are Driving Business Performance Across the Customer-Centric Enterprise, Executive Summary (September 2014), http://www.b2bnn.com/wp-content/uploads/2015/01/CMOC-Mastering-Executive-Summary_FINAL2_9-15-141.pdf, downloaded February 3, 2015.

4. A Winterberry Group White Paper: Marketing Data Technology: Cutting Through the Complexity (January 2015), http://www.iab.net/media/file/IAB_Winterberry_Group_White_Paper-Marketing_Data_Technology-January-2015.pdf, downloaded February 3, 2015.

5. Intel (August 2012) Big Data Analytics, http://www.intel.com/content/dam/www/public/us/en/documents/reports/data-insights-peer-research-report, date accessed February 4, 2015.

6. *Forbes* (April 2, 2012), Is Data The New Oil?, http://www.forbes.com/sites/perryrotella/2012/04/02/is-data-the-new-oil/

7 Light Touch

1. McKinsey (August 2013), Bullish on Digital: McKinsey Global Survey results, http://www.mckinsey.com/insights/business_technology/bullish_on_digital_mckinsey_global_survey_results, date accessed February 5, 2015.

2. Gartner (January 2012), By 2017 the CMO will Spend More on IT Than the CIO, http://my.gartner.com/portal/server.pt?open=512&objID=202&mode=2&PageID=5553&resId=1871515&ref=Webinar-Calendar (home page), date accessed November 3, 2014.

3. Accenture (2014), Accenture Interactive 2014 CMO-CIO Alignment Survey, http://www.accenture.com/us-en/Pages/insight-cmo-cio-alignment-digital-summary.aspx. (home page), date accessed November 5, 2014.

4. Accenture (2012), The CMO–CIO Disconnect, Bridging the Gap to Seize the Digital Opportunity, http://www.accenture.com/sitecollectiondocuments/pdf/accenture-2040-cmo-cio.pdf, downloaded January 5, 2015.

5. IBM (2014), The New Hero of Big Data and Analytics, http://www-01.ibm.com/common/ssi/cgi-bin/ssialias?infotype=PM&subtype=XB&htmlfid=GBE03607USEN#loaded, downloaded November 7, 2014.

6. Information Week (August 2014), Five Priorities for Chief Data Officers, http://www.informationweek.com/big-data/big-data-analytics/5-priorities-for-chief-data-officers/d/d-id/1297884.

7. Data Blueprint (2013), Unlocking Business Value, The Precarious State of the CDO: Insights Into a Burgeoning Role, http://datablueprint.com/publications/2013-The-Precarious-State-of-the-CDO.pdf, downloaded September 4, 2014.

8. Interview with Tom Buday by Norm Johnston (February, 2015).

9. Future Buzz Analytics (December 2013), Most Desirable Skill (And Largest Talent Gap) for 2014, http://thefuturebuzz.com/2013/12/04/analytics-most-desirable-skill-and-largest-talent-gap-for-2014/.

10. NOAA, "Enhancing Our Nation's Strength," http://www.noaa.gov/features/economic/economicstrength.html.

8 Through the Looking Glass

1. CCS Insight (August 2014), Smartwatches and Smart Bands Dominate Fast-Growing Wearables Market, http://www.ccsinsight.com/press/company-news/1944-smartwatches-and-smart-bands-dominate-fast-growing-wearables-market, date accessed February 2, 2015.

2. Technology Advice (September 30, 2014), Study: Wearable Technology & Preventative Healthcare, http://technologyadvice.com/medical/blog/study-wearable-technology-preventative-healthcare/.

3. Apple, https://developer.apple.com/app-store/review/guidelines/

4. *International Business Times*, IDTechEx (July 9, 2014), RFID Technology Market Set for Huge Growth, http://au.ibtimes.com/rfid-technology-market-set-huge-growth-1346517.

5. Packing-Gateway.com (December 16, 2009), RFID Tags Could Pose Threat to Recycling, http://www.packaging-gateway.com/news/news72615.html, date accessed December 2014.

6. RFID Insider (January 27, 2014), Baby, It's Cold Inside: Smart Appliances & RFID, http://blog.atlasrfidstore.com/baby-cold-inside-rfid-smart-appliances.

7. Interview with Mort Greenberg by Norm Johnston (February, 2015).

8. *Time* (August 2012), Your Wireless Life: Results of *TIME's* Mobility Poll, http://content.time.com/time/interactive/0,31813,2122187,00.html, date accessed January 5, 2015.

9. Center for the Digital Future (January 2012), Special Report: America at the Digital Turning Point, http://annenberg.usc.edu/News per cent20and per cent20Events/News/~/media/PDFs/CDF_DigitalReport.ashx, downloaded September 7, 2014.

10. Microsoft, The Right to Anonymity, http://advertising.microsoft.com/en-us/cl/4251/the-right-to-anonymity, date accessed February 16, 2014.

11. Gruppo Telecom Italia (August 13, 2014), Trusted Personal Data Management: A User Centric Approach, http://www.eitictlabs.eu/fileadmin/files/docs/documents_helsinki/FC_PersonalData_Oulu_13082014_ANTONELLI.pdf, downloaded September 4, 2014.

12. *The Financial Times* (February 18, 2013), Data Mining Offers Rich Seam, http://www.ft.com/cms/s/2/61c4c378-60bd-11e2-a31a-00144feab49a.html#axzz3UsNXN6C7.

13. eMarketer (March 14, 2014), Ad Fraud Remains a Moving Target, http://www.emarketer.com/Article/Ad-Fraud-Remains-Moving-Target/1010675.

14. MacRumors (February 10, 2015), Apple CEO Tim Cook Speaking Live at 2015 Goldman Sachs Technology Conference, http://www.macrumors.com/2015/02/10/cook-goldman-sachs-conference-2015/.

15. McKinsey (March 2013), McKinsey Quarterly: Big Data: What's your plan?, http://www.mckinsey.com/insights/business_technology/big_data_whats_your_plan.

Index